THE INTERCITY STORY

Euston station; gateway to the West Coast route and headquarters of an integrated InterCity business

THE *INTERCITY STORY*

Edited by Mike Vincent and Chris Green

Oxford Publishing Co.

Acknowledgements: One of the very real pleasures of editing a book such as this is the number of enthusiastic and supportive individuals with whom you find yourself working. I would therefore like to extend my heartfelt appreciation to all those who have contributed to this book and who have made my job so enjoyable and exciting.

My special thanks go to the railway and business authors who have produced individual contributions for the text: Richard Hope, Gary Smith, Roger Ford, Chris Heaps, John Gough, Alan Williams, Colin J. Marsden, Brian Perren, Michael Beswick, Sarah Burley, Chris Green, Ian Hurst and David Rollin.

In addition, past and present members of the InterCity Directors' Group have provided me with much help and support throughout the project but particular thanks are due to Geoff Ashton, Richard Brown, John Cimelli, Terry Coyle and Ivor Warburton for their critical and comprehensive comments. Original material from Cyril Bleasdale and Dr John Prideaux has been most helpful in the writing of Chapters Two and Three. At very short notice, Peter Semmens provided information for the train running logs contained in the InterCity Factfile and my special appreciation goes to him for that material.

A book of this scope requires a great deal of planning and checking. My thanks go to Brian Daniels, Malcolm Parsons, Ray Loft, Mike Carroll and Chris Austin for their painstaking work in this area. For achieving miracles in very tight timescales, special words of appreciation need to be given to the wonder workers who undertook the physical production of the book against impossible deadlines. Warmest congratulations must go to: InterCity's Public Affairs production team led by the indefatigable Dennis Lovett; to David French for his creativity with the cover design; to David Williams and all the hardworking staff at Acegraphics; to Leo Cooke, Mick Cooke and Martin Dorrell of Original Repro Limited at Oxford; to Colin Judge for compiling the index and for his strong production support; and the Oxford Publishing Company/Haynes for their vital role in the distribution of this unique book. Throughout the production period Elsa Redpath and Sarah Gibbs provided invaluable day-to-day support to the InterCity team that turned the vision of this book into hard reality.

Finally my thanks go to all those InterCity staff who over the years have made 'The InterCity Story' truly come to life.

Mike Vincent
Bath 1994

Photographers: The photographs in this book are the creative work of a talented team.
They are: Peter Alvey (Milepost 92½), John Byrne, Phil Caley, Alan Cheek (InterCity), Michael J. Collins, Chris Dixon, Colin Garratt (Milepost 92½), Colin J. Marsden, Brian Morrison, Gavin Morrison, Dick Riley, Peter J. Robinson, Jane Towers (Milepost 92½) and John Whiteley.
We also acknowledge the use of library material from: Aerofilms, British Broadcasting Corporation, BRB Photo Archive (held by Milepost 92½), British Library (Newspaper Library), Colour Rail, E.M.A. (Daily Telegraph), Lens of Sutton, Milepost 92½, Millbrook House, Mirror Group Newspapers, National Railway Museum (T. E. Williams collection), National Railway Museum (Poster Library), Press Association (Photo Library), Quadrant Picture Library (Autocar), Quadrant Picture Library (Anthony R. Dalton), Times Newspapers.

CONTENTS

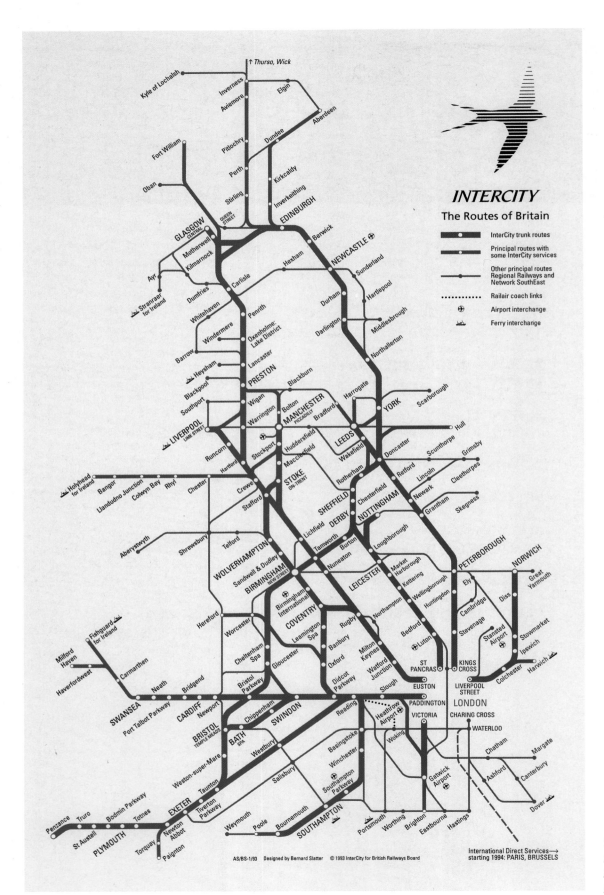

INTERCITY

The Routes of Britain

InterCity trunk routes

Principal routes with
some InterCity services

Other principal routes
Regional Railways and
Network SouthEast

Railair coach links

Airport interchange

Ferry interchange

↑ *Thurso, Wick*

Kyle of Lochalsh
Inverness
Aviemore
Elgin
Aberdeen
Fort William
Pitlochry
Dundee
Oban
Perth
Kirkcaldy
Stirling
Inverkeithing
GLASGOW CENTRAL
QUEEN STREET
EDINBURGH
Ayr
Motherwell
Kilmarnock
Berwick
Stranraer for Ireland
Dumfries
Carlisle
Hexham
NEWCASTLE
Whitehaven
Penrith
Sunderland
Durham
Hartlepool
Windermere
Oxenholme Lake District
Darlington
Middlesbrough
Barrow
Lancaster
Northallerton
Heysham
PRESTON
Blackburn
Blackpool
Harrogate
Scarborough
Southport
Wigan
Bolton
Bradford
YORK
Liverpool LIME STREET
Warrington
MANCHESTER PICCADILLY
Hull
Runcorn
Huddersfield
LEEDS
Doncaster
Scunthorpe
Grimsby
Stockport
Wakefield
Holyhead for Ireland
Bangor
Llandudno Junction
Colwyn Bay
Rhyl
Chester
Crewe
Hartford
Macclesfield
Rotherham
Retford
Lincoln
Cleethorpes
Stafford
STOKE ON TRENT
SHEFFIELD
Chesterfield
Newark
Aberystwyth
Shrewsbury
Telford
Lichfield
DERBY
NOTTINGHAM
Grantham
Skegness
WOLVERHAMPTON
Tamworth
Burton
Loughborough
PETERBOROUGH
NORWICH
Sandwell & Dudley
Nuneaton
Market Harborough
Great Yarmouth
Hereford
BIRMINGHAM NEW STREET
LEICESTER
Kettering
Ely
Diss
Milford Haven
Worcester
Birmingham International
Rugby
Wellingborough
Cambridge
Stowmarket
Haverfordwest
Carmarthen
Cheltenham Spa
COVENTRY
Northampton
Huntingdon
Stevenage
Stansted Airport
Ipswich
Neath
Bridgend
Gloucester
Leamington Spa
Banbury
Bedford
KINGS CROSS
Colchester
Harwich
SWANSEA
Port Talbot Parkway
Bristol Parkway
Oxford
Milton Keynes
Luton
ST PANCRAS
LIVERPOOL STREET
CARDIFF
Newport
Chippenham
Didcot Parkway
Watford Junction
EUSTON
PADDINGTON
Margate
BRISTOL TEMPLE MEADS
SWINDON
Slough
LONDON
Chatham
BATH SPA
Westbury
Reading
Heathrow Airport
VICTORIA
CHARING CROSS
Weston-super-Mare
Basingstoke
Woking
WATERLOO
Canterbury
Taunton
Salisbury
Winchester
Gatwick Airport
Ashford
EXETER
Tiverton Parkway
Weymouth
Southampton Parkway
Brighton
Dover
Penzance
Truro
Bodmin Parkway
Totnes
Newton Abbot
Poole
Bournemouth
Portsmouth
Worthing
Eastbourne
Hastings
St Austell
PLYMOUTH
Torquay
Paignton
SOUTHAMPTON

AS/BS-1/93   Designed by Bernard Slatter   © 1993 InterCity for British Railways Board

International Direct Services→
starting 1994: PARIS, BRUSSELS

*The final route
map produced
by the InterCity
business in 1993*

Foreword

BY CHRIS GREEN

MANAGING DIRECTOR, INTERCITY (1992-94)

In less than a generation, InterCity has grown from a train name to become one of Britain's largest and best known service industries with a £1 billion turnover. It has transformed itself from a nationalised industry with a subsidy, into Europe's only profitable passenger rail business. We have written this book for those people who are interested in InterCity's history, its marketing, its business turnround and its leadership.

It has been written by a team of InterCity managers and well-known railway writers. It thus offers a unique and authoritative perspective of InterCity as seen from both inside and outside the organisation. Its early chapters provide a detailed history whilst its later chapters develop key themes such as marketing, design, rolling stock, catering and caring for the customer. The final chapter predicts how the InterCity brand could act as the torch for the newly created train companies in an uncertain future. Appendices offer a permanent record of useful dates, facts and figures.

The book tells the story of rail's fight against the post-war growth of the car, express coaches and domestic airlines. It explains how InterCity has managed to spend the last six years in profit – a unique performance in Europe. It is also the story of a marketing brand that not only made itself a household name in Britain but has gone on to give its name to most of Europe for civilised, high speed rail travel.

Since I joined British Rail in 1965, my own railway career has intertwined with InterCity at various times and in various places. It was therefore a tremendous honour to become Managing Director of a lively InterCity team from 1992 to 1994 just as InterCity was becoming a unified national business with its own balance sheet, assets and staff.

The InterCity Story must rank as one of the greatest achievements of British Rail during the post-war era. It is a team story involving the motivation and dedication of 30,000 staff. I hope that you will enjoy reading it.

We offer it with pride.

Chris Green

March 1994

InterCity Luxury Land Cruises provide a delightful mixture of inspiring scenery and catering excellence

Preface

BY RICHARD HOPE
CONSULTANT EDITOR,
RAILWAY GAZETTE INTERNATIONAL

"They must have cooked the books – nobody carries passengers at a profit" was the reaction of one European railway president on hearing that InterCity had earned £57m on an £840m turnover in 1988-89, its first year as a commercial business. But then Alfred E Perlman, President of Penn Central Railroad, had assured me twenty years earlier that it was "quite impossible" to operate Japan's new Tokaido line linking Tokyo with Osaka at a profit, let alone pay off the cost of the new line.

Today, it is widely acknowledged that the Tokaido Shinkansen and the initial TGV route from Paris to Lyons completed in 1983 were profitable investments by any standard – though the same cannot be said of some other high speed lines. InterCity's astonishing achievement in recording a profit in every one of the six years from April 1988 to March 1994 has never gained such widespread recognition. The miracle is still not truly believed by many in Britain, let alone abroad. I hope *The InterCity Story* will help to put that right.

Sceptics may question whether InterCity was earning enough to renew assets, or was being propped up through subsidy being paid to Regional Railways and Network SouthEast. The fact is that BR had developed accounting and cost allocation systems as good or better than those available to any other national railway operator. A rigorous attempt was made to treat InterCity as a commercial business. If anything, InterCity bore more than its fair share of costs as prime user, or owner, of trunk routes like the West Coast Main Line.

But there is far more to the InterCity story than mere accounting. What emerged on BR in the 1960s was a completely new approach to the provision of express services between cities 100 to 400 miles apart, using infrastructure built in the nineteenth century.

When the West Coast route out of Euston was electrified to Manchester, Liverpool and Birmingham in 1966-67, the timetable pattern and frequency bore more resemblance to a suburban railway than a traditional main line of that era. In place of occasional moderately fast expresses interleaved between slower trains at random times, hourly or even half-hourly services of fixed formation headed north 5 minutes apart at a uniform line speed of 100 mph.

Given the background of the time, it was a remarkable development. In the mid-1960s Britain's rail network was shrinking by as much as 1,000 miles in a single year. Motorways and air were seen as the transport of the future. The West Coast electrification south of Crewe was delayed by a viability review and only allowed to go ahead after economies were found; hence the survival of mechanical signalboxes on the Trent Valley Line.

Even so, by 1965 a team of BR economists charged with defining a rail network that could operate as a commercial business was suggesting that potential demand between London and Manchester could be met most economically by a single daily train of 20 coaches. They saw no future for the East Coast main line north of Newcastle, where the 100 mph 'Deltic' diesels were already making a major impact on revenue.

Above all, it was the surge of new business that the nascent InterCity services generated, coupled with a change of government and the 1968 Transport Act, that swept such negative thinking into the dustbin before it could influence the British Railways Board's policy.

With the 1970s came the diesel High Speed Train, soon renamed Inter-City 125. By 1979, BR's timetable showed a best average speed between advertised stops of 106 mph compared to only 110 mph on the Shinkansen, leaving other countries, including France, well behind. The world sat up and took notice.

Imitation, they say, is the sincerest form of flattery. Today, the InterCity brand name – either rendered in English in various forms or just as IC – can be found in the timetables of Norway, Sweden, Denmark, Germany, Poland, the Netherlands, Belgium, Austria, Slovakia, Switzerland, Italy, Spain and Portugal, not to mention New Zealand, New South Wales and Cameroun.

The fact that the IC label elsewhere does not always relate to BR's concept of fast, regular-interval trains offering high quality service to First and Standard should not detract from this well-deserved recognition of the basic merit of what BR's InterCity business has actually achieved.

Since 1979, InterCity has spread the benefits of speed rather than raised the ceiling; the record 106 mph start-to-stop still stood in 1993 within the 125 mph maximum, but performance on the Midland main line, for example, had dramatically improved. Meanwhile, France, Germany and Spain had built new lines and thus pulled ahead of BR. Yet InterCity's timetables are so intensive that in 1991 more trains were run at 100 mph or more in Britain than in any other European country.

To turn speed into profit requires commercial acumen. InterCity faced a tough challenge in the most deregulated transport market in Europe. However, the fact that it enjoyed a large measure of freedom to set fares according to the market, when most other railways were (and some still are) applying a standard rate per kilometre, was crucial.

Latterly, InterCity has progressed to yield management and made great strides in customer care. These are very much current themes for the 1990s as the new train operating companies prepare themselves for privatisation. Preservation of the InterCity brand name, in which so much capital has been invested with remarkable success in terms of public awareness, remains the aim though none can say at this juncture what will actually happen to it. Should the Government's ultimate intent be to introduce outright competition between franchised and open access operators come about, it is hard to see how a single brand name can survive. Time will tell.

Along with the brand name go economies of scale in terms of marketing a national network rather than half-a-dozen individual routes, and the customer's perception of a quality service that covers the country. Here is another area where political promises about the retention of network benefits conflict with the basic strategy of fragmentation and competition underlying the Government's privatisation plan.

Of more immediate concern is investment. InterCity bequeaths to the new TOCs a rolling stock fleet of reasonable average age, and track that is basically in good shape, but there are some real time bombs ticking as regards signalling. The Government wants the private sector to assume the risk involved in investing both in trains and infrastructure. This might imply acceptance by manufacturers of maintaining their equipment during its predicted working life; but it could mean accepting full commercial risk, where financial rewards are linked to revenue earned by the assets.

What we do know is that current levels of investment in InterCity are under 40% of the £225m a year needed to sustain present services indefinitely. Predictions and promises of investment to come in the next few years are not an alternative for contracts which should be awarded now, but which are not being progressed because of the confusion and uncertainty surrounding privatisation.

Let us be clear on at least one point. Customer care, yield management and the rest of the software which InterCity has sought to develop (and the private sector is supposed to do much better) is no substitute for adequate investment in modern technology.

Rail's share of the passenger market is 35% in Japan, around six to ten per cent in Western Europe (with Britain at the low end of the range) and less than 1% in North America. A pessimist would diagnose failure. An optimist would see immense scope for growth in Europe if only the product was right.

Cars and planes may not have much in the way of higher speeds in prospect, but the former offers continually rising comfort at static or falling real cost, while airlines have scope for cutting time spent on the ground – if only through fast rail links to city centres like Heathrow Express. Unless InterCity develops technically as well as renewing assets, it must eventually fail.

There are interesting parallels between the mid 1990s and the mid 1960s, as well as important differences. Rail investment is currently plunging from a peak, especially if one excludes ongoing preparations for the Channel Tunnel, such as the purchase of Eurostar trains. Rail freight is in steep decline. In John MacGregor, as in Ernest Marples, we have a transport minister who is privately sceptical of rail's value and wants to switch funds from public transport to roads.

The biggest differences lie in public attitudes to rail, and in our closer ties with Europe. In the 1960s, before *The InterCity Story* really started, the public basically saw railways as obsolete. Back in 1958, I wagered £10 that there would still be two daily trains between London and York in 1988 – and subsequently collected my winnings, sadly depleted by inflation. In the 1950s, with steam still dominant, it was an act of faith; by 1962, when I left the railway industry for two years because the future under the chairmanship of Richard Beeching looked so bleak, such a bet would have seemed positively reckless. In the year that the Channel Tunnel opens at last, what odds would the bookies now have on offer on complete closure of the East Coast main line before 2024?

The start-up of the Eurostar service from London to Paris and Brussels will highlight with embarrassing clarity the different attitudes to rail investment on opposite sides of the Channel. Surveys continue to show that this investment gap is widening, with Britain near the bottom of the West European league. Meanwhile, there is growing pressure within the European Union to make much greater use of rail so as to alleviate road and air congestion.

Perhaps the biggest difference of all between 1964 and 1994 lies in the public statements of ministers. Then, closure of all unprofitable railways (including some busy commuter routes) was deemed an acceptable objective. Today, the declared aim of privatisation is a reduction in taxpayer support but subject to the more important objective of a busier network offering even better services.

The great mystery for InterCity is how the switch is to be made from yesterday's profitable but seriously underfunded network to a number of independent franchised operations which will attract more custom and adequate investment. Remember that they will depend on Railtrack, the national infrastructure owner, not only for day-to-day performance, but also for the kind of total route modernisation that we saw on the East Coast Main Line in the 1980s and which is so conspicuously absent from the West Coast in the 1990s.

Will it work, and if so, how will it work? In search of comfort, we should perhaps look back to 1948 when the railways were not merely nationalised, but merged with other transport modes into a monstrous bureaucratic structure that quickly proved unworkable. Professionals in the industry threatened disaster. My predecessor as editor of *Railway Gazette,* John Kay, reputedly threatened to cease publication at the end of 1947 because he thought that there would be nothing worth writing about!

In truth, the early years were not easy for the nationalised railway. Restructurings came thick and fast, a process that never ceased to this day. Yet out of the conflict and gloom of the Beeching era came the flowering of InterCity, now widely admired and imitated throughout Western Europe.

I believe that 30 years hence Britain will have a modern InterCity network in place with strong links to the Continent. My belief rests quite simply on the knowledge that this is actually happening everywhere in Europe. Now that we are no longer an island, Britain surely cannot take a quite different course? Because our trunk routes are well aligned, the case for new lines is said to be weak – apart from the Channel Tunnel link to London. This may prove to be true if maximum speeds on the older lines can be raised to 160 mph, perhaps with tilting trains. But some new building will be essential.

In between, the crystal ball is opaque. Experience is no guide because nobody has attempted to run railways in the vertically and horizontally fragmented way that is now envisaged. Whatever our personal predictions are for the next 10 years, there are perhaps only two certainties; the first is that the prediction will be wrong because events will take some unsuspected turn, and the second is that there will be plenty to write about. **" ,**

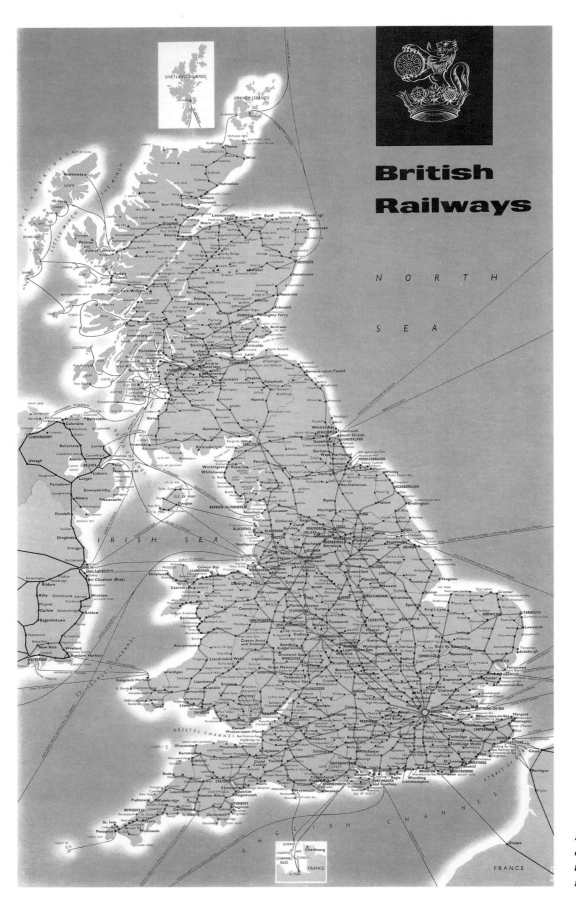

British Railways 1956 corporate map showing the density of the rail network at that time

Chapter One
INTERCITY'S ROOTS
THE 1950S AND 1960S

The first "Inter-City" – hauled by a 'King' Class locomotive in 1959

The term 'Inter-City,' or 'InterCity' as it became from the early 1980s, conjures up a picture of high profile, high quality, customer-focused passenger railway. This chapter sets out to explore the formative years of InterCity in the 1950s and 1960s when so many of the seeds sown were reaped with such success in the following decades. It looks back to the radical nationalisation of 1948 and through to the commercialism of the Beeching era which finally launched the InterCity we know today.

InterCity began in earnest in 1966 when it became the product name of the new electric expresses between London, Liverpool and Manchester. An historic perspective of the intervening years offers a fascinating pattern of

evolution culminating in a profitable £1 billion turnover business in the 1990s.

The 1950s and 1960s provided the seed-bed for InterCity in a slow and disjointed period of gestation. The 1970s accelerated the growth in every sense of the word with the development of the world famous High Speed Train (or HST) which provided InterCity with both an identity and a means to beat the competition. The 1980s saw InterCity establishing itself as a profitable marketing sector and brand alongside its sisters, Network SouthEast and Regional Railways. Finally, the 1990s saw InterCity reaching its fulfilment as a self-contained business within British Rail with its own balance sheet, assets, staff and marketing.

THE
INTER-CITY

MONDAYS TO FRIDAYS

NORTHBOUND			SOUTHBOUND		
LONDON (PADDINGTON)	dep	9 0 am	WOLVERHAMPTON (LOW LEVEL)	dep	4 25 pm
HIGH WYCOMBE	dep	9A35 am	BIRMINGHAM (SNOW HILL)	dep	4 50 pm
BIRMINGHAM (SNOW HILL)	dep	11 15 am	LEAMINGTON SPA (GENERAL)	dep	5 20 pm
WOLVERHAMPTON (LOW LEVEL)	arr	11 35 am	HIGH WYCOMBE	arr	6B30 pm
			LONDON (PADDINGTON)	arr	7 5 pm

A Stops to take up passengers only
B Stops to set down passengers only

BRITISH RAILWAYS

*The first train to carry the Inter-City name was this 1950
express from Paddington to Wolverhampton and return*

It would have been a small step to complete the logical process with the privatisation of the total InterCity business. It was certainly considered, but the 1993 Railways Act determined that InterCity should instead be broken back into the individual routes which had formed it. History is often circular and there may well be lessons for future pioneers as we begin our exploration of the seeds of the InterCity business in the postwar decades of the 1950s and 1960s.

The pre-Beeching 1948-1961 period

InterCity as we know it began in earnest in the Beeching era of the 1960s. It is, however, important to set the 1960s in their historic perspective with a quick look at express train operations before and after the second world war.

It is important to note that the British railway system did not develop as a planned and unified network. It grew instead from an unplanned explosion of small, competing private ventures. The InterCity network of 1994 represented the extreme change to a single, national product of consistent, high speed services across the country. How did this dramatic change come about?

By the outbreak of the first world war in 1914, a clearly identifiable pattern of train services had grown up with key main lines serving the principal centres of population. Express trains plied those main lines whilst stopping services served all stations. A number of semi-fast services fitted uneasily between the other two categories, often running to no clear pattern. Nonetheless, it seems fair to say that by 1923 when over 100 railway companies amalgamated into the 'Big Four' – the Great Western Railway (GWR), the London, Midland & Scottish Railway (LMSR), the London & North Eastern Railway (LNER) and the Southern Railway (SR) – Britain had achieved faster, more frequent inter-city services than its continental counterparts.

Exhausted and starved of investment after the enormous strains and demands placed upon them by the second world war, the railways were nationalised on 1st January 1948. Not only were main line railways nationalised within the transport portfolio, but so were certain elements of road freight, bus operation, canals and London Transport (both buses and underground railways). The British Transport Commission was formed to administer the whole enterprise, with a Railway Executive to manage the railways. Day to day rail operations were in the hands of six Regional Boards – organised geographically – whilst the whole complex series of organisations traded as British Railways.

At last, the opportunity seemed to have arrived in the 1950s to have a long, hard look at the railway system and

*This was how 'The Times' reported nationalisation of the
railways on 1st January 1948*

THE TIMES THURSDAY JANUARY 1 1948

...ES INCREASED IN FRANCE	STATE-OWNED RAILWAYS	THE NEW HONC...

...AL REFORM

STATE-OWNED RAILWAYS

POLICY OF THE COMMISSION

SIR C. HURCOMB'S OUTLINE

...OF WEALTH" ...SSESSED

ONE VIS... FOUF...

O.M. FO'...

Own Correspondent

PARIS, DEC. 31

...ures, most of them pro-ease of taxation in some ...ontinue to be rolled out of Assembly like news-printing press. It took ...ght for the Assembly ...he next three months 116m.) for ordinary and of 32,000m. ...traordinary military ...nclude all services ...s of the French

...: fiscal reform were a new scale for the external signs of ...uer will be presumed ...t six times that of the ...ises he inhabits.: to ...0 francs (£200) for ...and 120,000 francs ...al woman servant: one man servant and each additional man ...16) for each horse-

increase in the in-...lcohol, spirits, and ...etween 4s. 8½d. and out 4s. a gallon. All ...ax of 100,000 francs

...for a special levy ...aving been knocked ...onal Assembly, was by the Council of

...efore midnight the the 1948 Budget, francs (£1,875m.), he minority repre-nist.strength in the

From to-day the familiar monogram and initials which have denoted each of the four main-line railway companies since the amalgamations of 1923 will begin a quiet passage into disuse. Though the letters may remain for a time they will mark an era that has gone, for to-day British railways pass to the control of the State. No formal ceremonies will mark the handing over of the railways to the British Transport Commission, and the traveller will notice no change. It will be some time also before new markings and colours are decided upon.

In place of the four separate headquarters of the former companies there are now two central organisations: the British Transport Commission and the Railway Executive Committee.

The executive will operate from offices in Marylebone, under the chairmanship of Sir Eustace Missenden, formerly general manager of the Southern Railway. Other members of the executive are:—General Sir William Slim (public relations, stores, estate), Mr. W. P. Allen (staff and labour negotiations and welfare), Mr. David Blee (passenger, freight, and commercial development), Mr. V. M. Barrington-Ward (operating and marine), Mr. J. C. L. Train (civil engineering and signalling), and Mr. R. A. Riddles (mechanical and electrical engineering). Sir Wilfrid Ayre and Mr. C. Nevile are part-time members who will assist mainly in the commercial relations.

MAIN PRINCIPLES

The relations between the various controlling bodies was explained in a statement yesterday by Sir Cyril Hurcomb, chairman of the British Transport Commission. He says that the reorganization of railway administration is

The New to-day ann viscount, t lors, and . baronets. the Order given for August 14 ence of po The Duc' of Kent, Athlone are of the Roy tess Mour India, is adv Lord F National C barony to among the n Royal Air Fc after a brilli war, becam Military Go John Colvil 1943-47, Si mentary Priv of State fo Government. chairman of mittee, also t

ORI...

Literature ment of the T. S. Eliot, p and the Com Miss V. Sav Harold Ni and novelist. the first wor appointed ? The new W. I. McK

to see how best it might be brought together into a coherent whole. This could have included the birth of a national express InterCity network of services but the opportunity was missed for a decade. Perhaps, because the railways paid their way until 1952, the unique chance to take a close look at the opportunities for national networks and marketing were not truly grasped. However, the small profit swiftly turned into an ever-growing loss which eventually led, some ten years later, to the publication of the Beeching Report in the early 1960s and to the creation of the early InterCity services as a means of returning to profit.

To bring about economies in scale, it was planned that all equipment would be purchased in large quantities and could be used, as appropriate, anywhere in the country. It was intended that the standard designs of locomotives and coaches would draw together the best operational practices of the 'Big Four' railways and in April 1948 a series of comparative trials of pre-nationalisation locomotives were held in order to obtain the optimum designs for BR's range of standard classes.

At the same time a standard coach was commissioned which was to become the ubiquitous Mark I vehicle. Designed to be able to travel over most lines throughout the country, the standard body shell could accommodate all types of interiors from First and Third (later renamed Second) Class, to catering facilities, sleeping cars and parcel vans. With the introduction of these coaches, the 'buckeye' automatic coupling gave greater rigidity throughout the train when running and helped to prevent

serious damage in the event of an accident. The first standard locomotives and coaches appeared in 1951.

The 1955 Modernisation Plan

By the mid 1950s, major investment in the railways was essential if an express passenger network was to have any hope of surviving into the future. In January 1955 the Chairman of the Railway Executive, Sir Brian Robertson, finally published a £1,200m Modernisation Plan which would take 15 years to complete and which, he believed, would totally revolutionise the whole railway system and which laid the foundation stones for InterCity in the 1960s. The key features of this Plan were the abolition of the steam locomotive in favour of diesel and electric traction, electrification where density of traffic could justify the heavy initial investment required, improvements to track to permit higher speeds together with the extension of colour-light signalling, track circuiting and automatic warning systems (AWS) controlled from new power-operated signal boxes. There was to be a total modernisation of the rolling stock fleets and considerable expenditure on stations and parcels' depots.

Until the mid-1950s electrification schemes had been based on medium voltage, direct current systems, but post-war developments in France established 25kV alternating current as a more efficient system which was becoming adopted as standard for new projects in

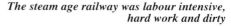

The steam age railway was labour intensive, hard work and dirty

TRAINS 8 MIN. EARLY ON ELECTRIFIED ROUTE

TIMINGS MAY BE REVISED

DAILY TELEGRAPH REPORTER

HINTS that British Railways would have to revise timetables on the London-Manchester-Liverpool link were given yesterday as the first trains on the newly electrified route arrived up to eight minutes early.

Delighted British Railway officials were surprised by the time cuts. One senior London Midland Region official said that the timings were likely to be reviewed at the end of the summer.

The fastest train completes the Manchester-London run in 2hr 35min, more than an hour quicker than before.

One train arrived at Euston yesterday almost 15 minutes early. It was held up because no platform was available.

£175m project

Mrs. Castle, Minister of Transport, joined in the praise for the £175 million project at a lunch to celebrate the inauguration of the electric services.

The fact that the scheme had been completed ahead of schedule was a triumph in itself, but she wondered how many people were aware of the revolution.

She asked: "When are we going to have peace from the knockers and moaners who continually decry our rail services?"

Some pruning of the rail system remained to be done. "This does and remove the depressing handicap of a permanent deficit.

Mrs. Castle made no reference to the liner train conflict with the National Union of Railwaymen. But Mr. Stanley Raymond, chairman of the British Railways Board, was optimistic that "we shall soon get over our difficulties."

Passengers on the early intercity trains were full of praise for a "smooth 100 m.p.h. ride." One Manchester woman made the trip for a day's shopping and a businessman chased a ticket collector to get his ticket back "for a souvenir."

London Day by Day—P16

1,800 PROTESTS AT THREAT TO RAIL LINE

Daily Telegraph Reporter

Protests by 1,800 local residents

BEA to fight 'service' war with railways

DAILY TELEGRAPH REPORTER

BRITISH EUROPEAN AIRWAYS is to wage a war over customer service with British Railways in an attempt to win, and keep, passenger traffic on the main routes in Britain.

In an article in the airline's staff magazine Mr. Anthony Milward, chairman of B.E.A. refers to "intense competition" which will face the company in the coming year.

"This is a fact, not a complaint. Our results to a great extent must depend on the nation's economy. I certainly see no reason to feel despondent: our traffic seems to be getting off to a good start and forward bookings look healthy."

He says the new rail service from London to Manchester is "very impressive.

"But the timing city centre to city centre, is not greatly different from that of B.E.A., so the winner will, to a great extent, be the operator who gives the best personal service. Let us be sure that that means B.E.A."

He states that B.E.A. will be offering some three million seats on its four "mainline" routes within Britain during the next 12 months.

O'NEILL REJECTS ALL-IRELAND PARLIAMENT

Daily Telegraph Reporter

Northern Ireland totally rejects

This report from the 'Daily Telegraph' of 19th April 1966 enthused on the excellence of the new electric service

mainland Europe. One of the best long-term decisions for InterCity was the 1955 agreement to adopt the new 25kV ac system for all future main line electrification. The Modernisation Plan still called for an extension of the existing systems around London, but new electrification in the Glasgow suburbs and on the whole of the West Coast main line of the London Midland Region from London to Manchester and Liverpool via Stoke on Trent and Crewe, was to be on the 25kV ac system. With considerable foresight, electrification of the Eastern Region main line from London to Leeds via Doncaster was also recommended but this work was deferred and did not actually start until the mid 1980s.

West Coast electrification

Work began immediately on the London Midland route and, being new technology, design and construction took some time. However, in 1960, the first section of the 'New Railway' from Crewe to Manchester began operation. The other northern section, from Crewe to Liverpool, was commissioned in 1962 and work gradually extended southwards towards London throughout the early 1960s. In the meantime, the other main plank of the Modernisation Plan was taking shape in the delivery of main line diesel locomotives for the rest of the UK network.

One of the West Coast electrics passes an almost empty M1 motorway in the 1960s

BR STANDARD LOCOMOTIVES OF THE 1950s

Many standard components were used for the range of BR locomotives designed in the early days of nationalisation.

Class 7 4-6-2 Britannia Pacific for express passenger work

Standard 2-6-2 tank locomotive for branch line work

78xxx Class 2-6-0 for branch line freight and secondary passenger services

Although designed primarily for freight work, the Class 9F 2-10-0s were used on express trains, notably on the old Somerset & Dorset line from Bournemouth to Bath

An inter-city diesel unit leaves Edinburgh for Glasgow in the
1960s

The Torbay Express passes Twyford in 1961 hauled by a Class 42
Warship diesel-hydraulic locomotive

The first step to InterCity 125 - a Blue Pullman awaits departure from Bristol Temple Meads in 1963

The Blue Pullmans

In 1960 the so-called Blue Pullmans were introduced in their attractive and special blue and grey livery. Five complete trains were built with a 1,000hp diesel electric power car at either end of a rake of passenger coaches. The self-contained trains formed the first step along the path to the production of one of the most successful passenger trains in the world, the InterCity 125. The Blue Pullmans ran on fast, limited-stop schedules and offered air-conditioning, individually-adjusted venetian blinds at each window and meals served at every seat. A supplementary fare was payable in order to gain that exclusivity.

Both the London Midland and Western Regions operated Blue Pullmans, the former having First Class accommodation only. They provided an early morning service from Manchester to London via Derby and, in order to make full use of the trains with their quick turnround capability, were employed on midday journeys to Nottingham. The Western Region's trains had both First and Second Class seating and provided business services from Bristol, Wolverhampton and Birmingham to Paddington. In addition, the WR sets provided a daytime 'fill-in' service to Oxford.

Whilst the business concept behind the trains was very successful, the trains themselves were not. They were 'one-offs' in a world of growing standardisation and they were expensive to operate and maintain. The bogies began to

give a very rough ride after a period of service and the Blue Pullmans were withdrawn in 1973. Nonetheless, they had demonstrated a demand for superior customer service from specific sectors of the travelling public and had provided the inspiration for InterCity's diesel train of the future, the High Speed Train or InterCity 125 as it later became.

'Deltics' for the East Coast

As work progressed on West Coast electrification, BR decided to buy high-powered diesel locomotives for the East Coast route's passenger services between King's Cross, Leeds, Newcastle and Scotland. Faced with growing competition from the private car and the expanding network of domestic air services, the forward-thinking East Coast management felt that they could wait no longer for electrification in this competitive environment. Fortunately, some real foresight had been shown by the English Electric Company who had designed and built a new high-powered diesel prototype locomotive known as the 'Deltic' at their own financial risk. Way ahead of its time and its competitors, this remarkable machine was capable of cruising at 100mph on the long journeys between London and Scotland. The East Coast managers saw this as the ideal candidate to bridge the gap until the East Coast main line was eventually electrified.

Twenty two production models were built in total and the first of these 100mph locomotives began to appear on

East Coast services during 1961. With the start of the 1962 timetables, dramatic cuts were made to the times of all East Coast services. Over an hour was cut between King's Cross and Edinburgh to create new six hour schedules between London and Scotland. Although six hour timings had been achieved by the pre-war steam-hauled 'Coronation' train, that particular service had run just once a day, on Mondays to Fridays only with a special supplement payable. In 1962, the average timing of all the route's daytime trains was down to a little over six hours and none required a supplement.

Diesel power was shrinking journey times quite considerably. To raise train speeds between Paddington, Bristol, South Wales and the West of England, a fleet of diesel hydraulic locomotives had made it possible for the Western Region to phase out its steam locomotives and upgrade its services. As dieselisation spread, train services on other trunk routes such as St Pancras to Nottingham, Derby and Sheffield and Liverpool Street to Norwich were accelerated and upgraded. As yet though, standards of service and image varied significantly over BR's main routes. Something was needed to bring these different services together in a consistent, coherent and marketable kind of way. A major opportunity presented itself with the introduction of the new electric services from Euston to Liverpool and Manchester in 1966. Inter-City as a corporate brand name was about to be born.

In 1960, the Conservative Government had become increasingly concerned at the rising annual deficit of British Railways, and appointed the Stedeford Committee as a special advisory group to the Minister of Transport, Ernest Marples, to inquire into and report on the steadily worsening financial position of the railways. One member of that Committee was a certain Dr Richard Beeching, Technical Director of Imperial Chemical Industries Limited. Mr Marples believed Dr Beeching had just the right qualities to become the Chairman of British Railways. The incumbent Chairman, Sir Brian Robertson, was due to retire in May 1961, and Dr Beeching duly replaced him as Chairman of the new British Railways Board. His purpose was singularly clear. He was required to carry out a deep and searching investigation into every aspect of the railways' operations and finances.

The Beeching Era : 1961-1969
The InterCity story accelerated during the Beeching era when a radical Board was seeking radical means to beat the new competition from motorways, cars and domestic airlines. The Beeching Report was published in March 1963 and revealed that over half the mileage carried only 4% of the passenger miles. Very large sections therefore did not even cover their day-to-day operating costs, such as wages, fuel, etc let alone track, signalling and other maintenance costs. The other half of the system, on the other hand, had earnings which covered route costs by more than six times.

A Class 45 hauling Mark I coaches leaves London St Pancras for Nottingham in 1978

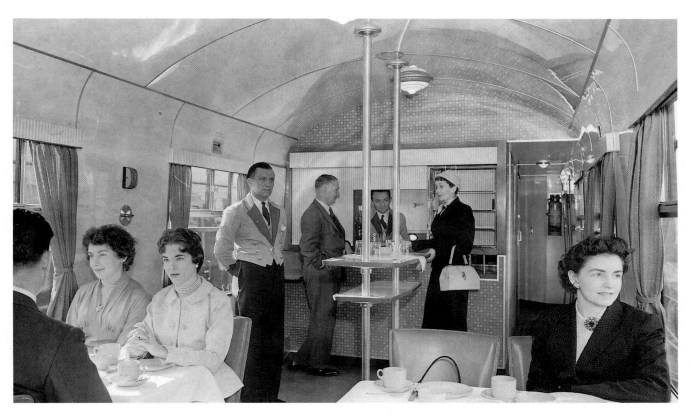

Compare this 1950s buffet with those of today

During the rebuilding of the West Coast main line, sleeper services used Marylebone as their London terminus

The Daily Mirror devoted five pages to the 'Beeching Report' on 28th March 1963

It was at last clear that the railway was at its best when concentrating on specific traffics such as fast passenger services, rather than trying to play the nineteenth century role of common carrier. Even with reduced operating costs which the rapidly spreading diesel traction was bringing – in some areas diesel railcar operation of local lines was cutting costs by up to 50% – there was no way in which many local and rural lines could ever be made viable. On the positive side, Beeching recommended that far more attention should be paid to the speed, reliability and comfort of the inter-city services which he believed should be provided by the fast and semi-fast trains at the expense of the local stopping services. Overall the Report suggested the closure of some 5000 route miles of track and 2000 stations. Many of the stopping services ran over lines used by express passenger trains and their removal would release track capacity to allow the higher speeds demanded for the inter-city services. Not all the proposed passenger closures were delivered but most were and at a pace that many considered to be indecent.

The Beeching era is an important period in the InterCity story. It was during that time that the importance of inter-city traffic for a forward-looking and potentially profitable railway was first clearly spelt out, even though the evidence for this state of affairs had long been available. It was in the Beeching era that the need for much finer, more precise costing procedures, which would enable the viability of much smaller parts of the

total operation to be assessed, was brought much more sharply into focus. Although fast inter-urban traffic has had a long and honourable place on the railway scene, it was really during the Beeching years that the foundations were put in place for today's intensive InterCity business.

The Inter-City name

The Beeching Report of 1963 was the first occasion when the term 'inter-city' was used to loosely describe the whole long-distance, express network. The specific words had first been used in a railway context on 25th September 1950 when the Western Region continued the GWR's tradition of giving names to its most prestigious trains by calling the 0900 from Paddington to Wolverhampton and its return, 'The Inter-City'. Following a revision of services over the route from Paddington to Birmingham and the North West, 'The Inter-City's' destination was extended to Chester in 1962. The name was then dropped in 1965 in anticipation of its adoption for the whole of the Euston to Liverpool and Manchester electric services the following year.

Another pioneering use of the word also came from BR's 1957 staff magazine when it stated that: 'The first of the new series of inter-city express diesel trains to enter service in Great Britain started work on the Glasgow to Edinburgh route on 7th January'. A series of diesel multiple units, built at Swindon in 1963 for services between Cardiff and Derby and Cardiff and Bristol were also described as 'inter-city' units. Indeed, the 1957 Annual Report of the British Transport Commission stated that it had been decided to provide three categories of express train called; Pullman de-luxe, special inter-city and ordinary express.

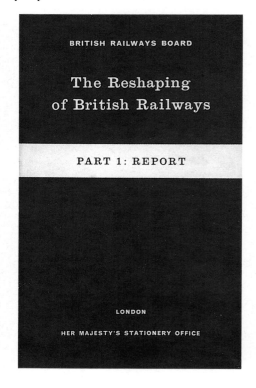

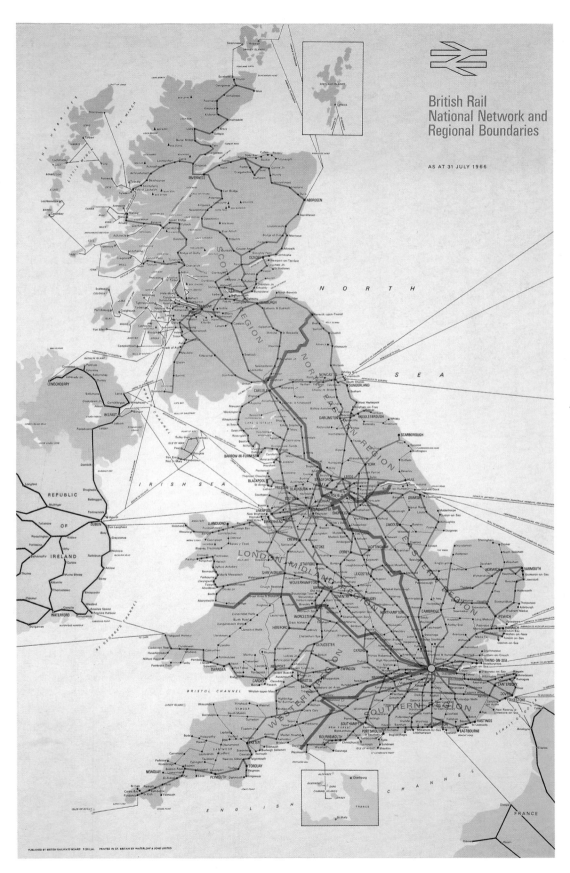

The publication of the Beeching Report had radically altered the system by the time this map appeared in 1966

11

The XP64 Prototype train incorporated many design features later to become standard on InterCity

BRB's Corporate Identity Programme 1965

One especially significant aspect for the InterCity story was Sir Brian Robertson's initiative in 1956 in forming a British Transport Commission Design Panel charged with advising on 'the best means of obtaining a high standard of appearance and amenity in the design of equipment'. The Design Panel influenced virtually every major development from then on.

A new corporate design initiative in 1965 launched a new BR image and the now world-famous and much emulated double arrow logo. Longer distance trains were now picked out in a distinctive blue and grey livery, whilst stopping trains were plain blue. This early recognition that long distance trains were different to other trains was the start of the idea which culminated in the sophisticated InterCity livery of the 1990s.

In 1963, the British Railways' workshops at Swindon had introduced a revised passenger coach bogie design. Designated B4 and capable of 100 mph, it had superior riding qualities to the ageing 90 mph Mark I coaches. At the same time, Swindon was also perfecting the associated Mark II coach body designs in which the whole body was built as a rigid box with no separate underframe. This radical design saved weight, gave extra rigidity and offered a safer environment compared to the Mark I type of 1951. The first of the new Mark II coaches came into extensive use on the 'New Railway' between Euston and the North West on its electrification in 1966 and completed the image of the rebirth of a modern, high speed railway complete with smart blue and grey livery.

In 1962 the British Railways Board authorised a further build of eight prototype coaches which were introduced in 1964 as the XP64 project.

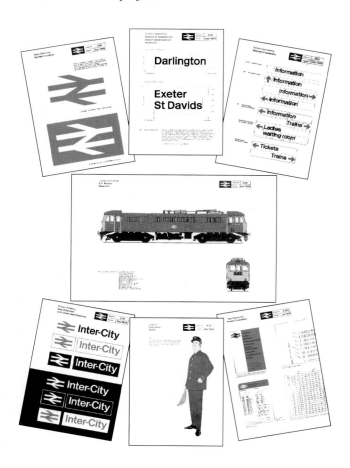

Macclesfield - a typically rebuilt station for the West Coast electrification

InterCity dateline – 1966

One of the most significant dates in the InterCity story is that of 18 April 1966 which was the inaugural day of the long-awaited electric services between Euston, Liverpool and Manchester. The new timetable was based on a consistent regular-interval concept and included journeys timed at an average of over 80 mph with sustained running at 100 mph for the first time ever in Britain. Stations were rebuilt including those at Manchester, Lichfield, Tamworth, Stafford and Euston.

The new service was an immediate success and demonstrated the phenomenon which came to be known as the 'sparks effect' – instant and sustained increases in passenger travel on newly electrified railways. The new service was such a success that additional trains had to be arranged to cope with the business. After just three months of the new service, traffic between Manchester, Liverpool and London was up by a remarkable 66% on the previous year. When the electrification was extended to Birmingham and Wolverhampton in March 1967 the results were equally dramatic and positive.

Instead of giving names to individual expresses as had been the practice previously, an historic decision was taken to brand the whole of the new service 'Inter-City' for promotional purposes. Promotion of the route also marked a major change in the practice of marketing and advertising in the railways. Instead of station posters preaching to the converted, television commercials, newspaper and magazine advertising and mailshots now delivered the message to the homes and offices of those who had seldom used railways. Specialist marketing teams were set up with many members recruited from outside the railway and external advertising agencies were increasingly used to improve professionalism. Since that time the skills of the marketeer have been central to the success of the InterCity operation.

The InterCity route electrification was extended via Birmingham in 1967 where it coincided with the total reconstruction of Birmingham New Street station. Here a new office was opened dealing with ticket sales, information, advance bookings and reservations, for both business and leisure travel. This was one of the first of a new type of Travel Centre, now taken-for-granted, yet so important to InterCity's future sales drive.

Political initiatives to put British Rail and its fledgling InterCity on a sounder business footing occurred in 1968 following the return of a Labour Government in 1964. Under the Transport Act of 1968, the Minister of Transport, Barbara Castle, announced an "11,000 mile basic railway network, which the Government and the British Railways Board have decided should be retained and developed". The accumulated deficit, of some £153 million, was written off. The 'social railway' was separated from the 'commercial railway', the government being prepared to support the 'social railway' and only for as long as it felt it was necessary. The intention was that 'commercial' businesses would move towards profit-ability and open competition but it was to take InterCity another 20 years to achieve that profitability against severe deregulated competition from coach and air.

Work began in 1966 on the first major national InterCity promotional campaign with the slogan *'Inter-City: Heart to Heart'*. This required 40 separate television commercials to highlight facilities in each area. This was the start of marketing all the principal long-distance routes which were at last starting to form themselves into a much more integrated network with its own identity. The new promotions increasingly used market research to establish customers' opinions and reactions. In 1968, a survey found a significant shift in public perception following the new InterCity network of services compared to those pre-1966. The spread of the new services was also an important factor in the public's new approval.

A key decision for InterCity's future competitiveness was made in 1969 when the Board announced that all new coaches to be built for InterCity would be air-conditioned regardless of class of travel. The transition to a fully air-conditioned fleet was to take twenty years to implement but it was to put the UK ahead of other world rail operators and gave it a vital edge in comfort and luxury which came to be recognised as part of rail's unique advantage for relaxed travel. Other railways were beginning to offer air-conditioning but usually in First Class coaches and usually with supplements payable. InterCity was uniquely farsighted in making air-conditioning standard in both First and Second Class and without supplements. It was to prove a highly successful decision in the competitive era of the 1980s.

In the same year a decision was made to market all Britain's sleeper services as a single InterCity Sleeper product. This followed a similar decision to create a national Motorail product for accompanied cars in 1966. In both cases the significance was the end of local regional promotions in return for the added-value of national product management. InterCity grew into its full strength from these early acts of national product management and branding.

The seeds of InterCity were undoubtedly sown in the 1950s and 1960s when the evolution began from the steam railway to the gradual but sustained advances in speed and business planning. Railways throughout Europe had started to encounter unprecedented levels of competition from other modes of transport. In order to fight back, the railways started to focus on exploiting the potential of their long distance, high speed services between major centres. From 1966 onwards, the InterCity concept had caught the public's imagination in Britain and had started along a path that would place it amongst the world's leaders in the provision of quality rail transport in the next decades. ✈

The Hull Pullman hauled by a Class 55 Deltic locomotive arrives at Kings Cross in June 1977

Fountainhall station lost its trains in 1969, when the line from Carlisle to Edinburgh via Hawick closed. The route was used by express trains from St. Pancras to Edinburgh

The newly opened M1 Motorway created competition for long distance journeys in the early 1960s

The BR Network map of 1975 highlighting the principal routes

Chapter Two

TECHNOLOGY FOR THE PEOPLE
1970-1982

A young passenger talks to the driver of a High Speed Train at King's Cross

In May 1970, InterCity's future as Europe's only profitable railway turned on one decision made at a meeting of the British Railways Board's Investment Committee. At that meeting, the Committee authorised £70,000 for the development of a prototype high speed diesel-electric train. Today we call that train InterCity 125. Its service history is distinguished by spectacular journey time reductions and a series of record runs which have all made it the fastest diesel train in the world. But, for the InterCity business, it was the train's earning power which was so decisive. With its unique blend of performance and comfort combined with steadily improving standards of on-board service, IC125 became a moneyspinner wherever it entered service.

However, unlike the much-publicised bullet trains in Japan, the TGV in France and the ICE trains in Germany, IC125 has achieved its success the hard way, running on existing rail routes laid down by the great Victorian engineers. IC125 was the uniquely British way to high speed and its development is the story of InterCity in the years of the 1970s.

High speed policy

By the end of the 1960s, there was agreement within BR that average journey times had to be reduced if the developing InterCity was to survive in a market where Government investment and technical development was favouring the car, the coach and the aeroplane. But the way forward to higher average speeds divided engineers and managers alike.

In December 1968, British Rail Research had finally received funding to develop its vision of an Advanced Passenger Train (APT) capable of running at up to 150 mph on existing track. The Government would provide half of the £4.8 million needed to produce a prototype train for trial running: BR would fund the other half.

The APT programme was set up independently of BR's established traction and rolling stock engineers who had launched the InterCity revolution back in the 1960s. It was, however, the latter group of engineers who had been intimately involved in the "sparks effect" of the London-North West electrification which had boosted ridership so dramatically by 66%. In partnership with the civil engineers, and with each new summer timetable, they were now reducing journey times on the East Coast route from London King's Cross to Edinburgh by using the high powered, high speed Class 55 Deltic diesel locomotives.

Nonetheless, however significant these developments were held to be by BR's engineers, their professional colleagues in the Research Division chose to see them as the work of yesterday's technology compared with their 150 mph, gas-turbine powered, tilting train. Their view was that while conventional technology chipped gently away at the minutes, APT would slash up to an hour from the longer runs.

A new technical vision

Then, in 1968, BR appointed a new Chief Engineer, Traction & Rolling Stock. His name was Terry Miller and he had the ideal pedigree to take conventional high speed trains into the 1970s. As a young man he had trained under the great railway engineer Sir Nigel Gresley who, with the development of the 'Silver Jubilee' on the LNER in the 1930s, had created the concept of the high speed, fixed-formation train. In the more recent past, Miller had been Chief Engineer of the Eastern Region of British Railways responsible for the mould-breaking Deltic diesels. Clearly, Terry Miller was the right person at the right time. He had the vision to see that conventional technology could build on the successes already experienced on the East and West Coast routes and he had the leadership ability to make major change happen again, and quickly.

A Class 55 Deltic hauled London express awaits departure from Leeds City in May 1976

The prototype HSDT Power Car undergoing testing at the Railway Technical Centre, Derby

It was also fortunate for Miller that much of the technology was already in place. His engineers had already begun to develop new coaching stock which was designed to replace the InterCity Mark II vehicles then in production. Significantly, and with considerable foresight, Miller had decided that this new stock should have the previously undreamed of design speed of 125 mph – about twice the legal road limit.

To be commercially viable, a new high speed train would have to be able to operate with the minimum number of changes to the existing track, structures, etc. One critical area that needed consideration was that of possible track damage incurred by trains travelling at higher speeds. The civil engineers specified that any new locomotive or power car would have to produce the same forces on the track at 125 mph as an existing 99 tonne Class 55 Deltic produced travelling at 100 mph. Fortunately, the far-sighted diesel engine builders, Paxman Engineering, had a new engine under development which would put 2,250 hp into a 68 tonne power car. This light weight would meet the civil engineers' track force requirements whilst, for the railway operators, two of these power cars would still take seven of the new Mark III coaches up to 125 mph.

Having dealt with the issues of running softly, safely and at high speed, it was also clearly important to consider the signal engineers' famous dictum of 'your right to speed is your power to stop'. As resignalling at that time was both impracticable and unaffordable, raising line speeds to 125 mph on existing track meant stopping within existing braking distances. Once again, in a fortuitous case of 'here's one we designed earlier', the right technology was available in the form of a British-designed disc brake allied with new anti-slide brake controls.

Production HST vehicles under construction

The prototype HSDT under test

A key decision

Meanwhile, the technical challenges of the APT programme were beginning to worry BR's commercial managers. So, when Terry Miller offered them a 125 mph train with a prototype up and running in just 22 months, the proposal to make this happen soon appeared before the British Railways Board. The then Chairman, Sir Henry Johnson, quickly became convinced that BR could not wait for APT to prove itself. At the same time, road and air competition continued to grow stronger. It was Johnson who expressed what was to become InterCity's traction and rolling stock philosophy for the next 20 years when he said: "We cannot stand still, we must go on improving track and trains on orthodox lines."

Once that decision was taken development of the new train accelerated. In August 1970 the development authorisation was changed to the construction of a prototype High Speed Diesel Train (HSDT) with six coaches and two power cars. In June 1972, the train which would take InterCity into the 21st century rolled out at Derby Works, as promised, just 22 months after authorisation and only a month after the experimental Advanced Passenger Train (APT-E) had appeared. Coincidentally, at the same time on the other side of the English Channel, French Railways unveiled the prototype Train à Grande Vitesse, the TGV. Interestingly, the British train would not only enter commercial service first but it would be the first to be sold abroad.

Tragically, a year of vital development was lost when both HSDT and APT were immediately boycotted by the trades' unions for having a single central seat in the cab with all the implications that the cab would be single-manned. But in many ways, the race between the two trains was already over. While the HSDT was a true prototype, fully equipped to run in revenue service, the APT-E was no more than a test train with only one part of one coach fitted out as a VIP saloon.

At this point, the stories of the two trains began to diverge. HSDT became a commercial success, thanks to heroic efforts on the part of the maintenance engineers and the manufacturers to overcome design weaknesses which had not been exposed by the truncated development testing process. On the other hand, APT ended up as a national disappointment; a bold strategic concept, starved of technical resources which should have developed into another winner alongside the HSDT but did not. InterCity was still paying the price on the West Coast in the 1990s.

HSDT on test

Once HSDT began running, its performance exceeded all expectations. For example, its disc brakes stopped it in 1,930 yards compared with the 2,200 yards allowed for a train travelling at 100 mph. In addition, its acceleration was better than hoped for and later on in its development it would be discovered that the train's aerodynamics were so good that another coach could be added to the original seven car formation without having to increase the output of the two power cars.

The prototype went to the East Coast main line for high speed trials. On 12th June 1973, it set a new diesel-powered world rail speed record of 143 mph whilst running on the fast, straight racetrack between York and Darlington. On the same line it also demonstrated an

Opened in 1972, Bristol Parkway was InterCity's first 'park and ride' station. This 1994 view shows the recently enlarged car park

The pre-production APT arrives at Euston after its inaugural run on 7th December 1981

The interior of the prototype HSDT set up in Pullman style

invaluable ability to get the train home on a single engine when failures occurred. On level track, the train can run at 110 mph on one power car thus maintaining a reasonable service.

When the Duke of Edinburgh opened the new National Railway Museum in September 1975, what better form of transport from London to York than the HSDT? Suddenly, however, in mid-journey the senior engineer on the train was called away from the official party. In one of the power cars a French-built circuit breaker had blown up. Would the same component do the same thing at the other end of the train? Fortune favoured InterCity and the journey was completed uneventfully – at least as far as the royal party was concerned.

Higher customer standards

For InterCity's customers this new technology has meant much more than shorter journey times. The Mark III coach, the cheapest and lightest steel-built air-conditioned coach in Europe, gives a quality of ride, even on poor track, that later designs have struggled to emulate. Whilst the internal ambience was not significantly better than that of the later models of the air-conditioned Mark IIe and IIf coaches, the positive overall impression for those 1970s customers, reinforced by the new buffet cars and the higher standards of on-board service, made the train a winner right from the start.

With electrification on the West Coast main line being extended to Preston, Carlisle and Glasgow and with the East Coast's route engineers still pulling further cuts in

journey times from their fleet of untiring 'Deltics', the Western Region's main lines to Bristol and South Wales were chosen to receive the first fleet of what were now to be simply called High Speed Trains or HSTs.

Built for speed

As part of a major upgrade for 125 mph operation, the Western Region's civil engineers, led by Chief Civil Engineer Phil Rees, turned Isambard Kingdom Brunel's great way west into a veritable billiard table and exploited its high speed potential to the maximum. Indeed, in some places so great were the changes to be made that only complete renewal of the track bed could meet the new standards required. Between Wootton Bassett (to the west of Swindon) and Bristol Parkway station, the track bed had to be blanketed with sand and polythene sheeting to restore effective drainage. Faced with the prospect of three years' disruption while this work was carried out under a series of weekend possessions, the decision was taken to shut the line down completely and do the work in five months. This entailed shift working around the clock during the summer of 1975 to get the work finished.

Brunel, of course, had been an early apostle of high speed and high levels of ride comfort and had, therefore, endowed the Great Western Railway's alignment with gentle gradients and sweeping curves. Building on this magnificent foundation and attending to some of the areas where Brunel's 19th century vision had actually faltered, Rees and his 20th century engineers improved upon the master's work, slewing the track to ease curves and raising line speeds wherever possible to the full 125 mph. Take the 112 miles between Paddington and Bristol

Parkway as an example. After the upgrading work had taken place only 14 miles would be run at less than 125 mph and all but two of those miles were at speeds over 100 mph.

With the prototype HSDT up and running, the 27 production trains for the Great Western main line on order and the infrastructure engineers hard at work, it was now time for the timetablers and marketeers to work out how InterCity was going to exploit fully its new assets. Pathing the 125 mph HST into the existing passenger and freight services was a major challenge but one which would get easier as successive fleets were introduced. The sheer performance of the HST reduced the impact of station stops and gave the operators something in hand. On one test run from Reading to Taunton, an HST gained eight minutes purely on its acceleration away from stops and speed restrictions.

The people's train

Hard though it may seem for us to believe today, one of the major concerns for the railway marketeers of 1975 was to persuade the everyday travelling public that a train like the HST was a train for them. High speed trains on other railways had almost invariably been sold as a premium product with business travellers prepared to pay a supplement for superior service and performance. In contrast, HST was InterCity's new standard product providing hourly, high speed services throughout the day. The concern was that ordinary members of the public would not perceive that such a train was for them.

Selling HST as the people's train meant playing down some of its features. Speed for speed's sake was out as were images of luxury travel. Instead the emphasis was on shorter journey times, greater comfort and improved on-board service. For business travellers, of course, there was no such resistance to a high quality service – in fact, it was long overdue. In the case of the Western Region services from London to Bristol and South Wales, the parallel M4 motorway had been abstracting traffic steadily. Now InterCity was striking back at the company car with a highly effective weapon. In 1975, as the production trains began to leave the works at Crewe and Derby, the HST had gained a new name. On the side of the power cars, the legend 'Inter-City 125' had appeared in large letters and figures. The marketing revolution had started.

The "nose cone" effect

On Monday, 4th October 1976, InterCity's high speed revolution began with a service of sixteen IC125s a day each way on the London-Bristol-Swansea routes. A decade earlier 70 mph had been considered the desirable commercial speed for InterCity trains. Now the fastest IC125 averaged just under 92 mph between Paddington and Bristol Parkway and much faster timings were to come. Nevertheless, in 1976, a 23 minute reduction on the

A production HST at work on the Western Region

best London-Cardiff time and a 15 minutes reduction off the London-Bristol trains were impressive enough to be getting on with and ridership began to climb. At a time of recession, the public responded with enthusiasm.

In the first six months of that service, ridership rose by 15% and in two years it was up by 33%. In the first two years of HST squadron service on the Western Region ten million passengers had been carried and business was up by a third on a highly competitive corridor. The economists had to coin a new phrase to describe the extraordinarily strong pulling power of the new train. InterCity 125 had been launched with the slogan "It's the changing shape of rail". Now its commercial impact was being dubbed the "nose cone" effect.

With the introduction of the May 1977 timetables, and with 82 services a day running at 125 mph, the twenty seven strong HST fleet was in full service. There was nothing to match this combination of speed and intensity anywhere in the world other than the Japanese Shinkansen. Meanwhile, as permanent way improvements were being completed, journey times continued to fall. Bristol Parkway was now only 70 minutes from Paddington on the fastest train, a start to stop average speed of 96 mph. On the South Wales route, the London to Cardiff time came down to 105 minutes.

Record runs

In 1977, Her Majesty Queen Elizabeth II celebrated the silver jubilee of her reign. For InterCity it was too good a chance to miss and so the Western Region decided to show that when it came to special runs the IC125 was in a class of its own. On 7th May 1977, a standard seven car train in the charge of Drivers W. Francis and R. Sandercock pulled out of Bristol Temple Meads Station bound for London. The aim of this run of the "Jubilee Special" was to average 100.1 mph. The train took just 68 minutes 19 seconds to arrive at Paddington – a start to stop average of 103.3 miles per hour without exceeding the 125 mph line limit.

On the return journey the train did even better. By Twyford, 31 miles out from Paddington, the average speed was 100 mph: by Bristol Parkway the average had gone up to 110 whilst, even after the slow run around the curves into Bristol, the start to stop average was 104.4 miles an hour. Not surprisingly, this was a world record for diesel traction.

In later years there would be even faster high speed runs culminating in the inauguration on 27th September 1985 of the new 'Tyne Tees Pullman' from Newcastle to London. As they would do with the launch of the electrified InterCity 225 some seven years later, the East Coast main line engineers and operators pulled out all the stops for what would be the ultimate demonstration of InterCity 125 performance. Considerable care went into the selection of the train for the run, even down to

Meeting of the prototypes: the prototype HSDT and APT-E stand together at Swindon during trials on Western Region

Three generations of East Coast motive power line up at York in March 1978. They are Gresley's A4 Pacific, a Class 55 Deltic and an InterCity 125

ensuring that the wheelsets were new to maximise the gearing. With the civil engineers having given special permission for the line speed to be raised to 140 mph in some key locations, the 268.6 miles to King's Cross was scheduled to be covered in 139 minutes.

By Darlington the train was already averaging 94 mph but, once on the East Coast route's superbly aligned racing ground between Darlington and York, the Pullman really flew. Cruising at over 130 mph, York was reached 2.5 minutes ahead of schedule at an average speed of 106.8 mph from Newcastle. By Grantham, the Pullman was ahead of its schedule by a further 3.5 minutes. However, the television cameras on board paid attention not to the schedule but more to the coffee slopping from a cup as even the excellent ride of the Mark III coaches was pushed to the comfort limit.

Then came Stoke bank where Sir Nigel Gresley's Class A4 locomotive 'Mallard' had set the world steam speed record of 126 mph. Racing down the bank speed rose to 142 mph before the slowing through Peterborough took place. And still there was no letting up. From Huntingdon to Hitchin the average speed was over 130 mph and King's Cross was reached some 9.5 minutes early at a start to stop average of 115.4 mph. Newcastle was potentially only 2 hours 9 minutes from London by rail!

Clearly, early fears that the travelling public would be deterred by high speed had been mistaken. The truth was that inside the long 23 metre Mark III coach the air suspension gave a soft, floating ride whilst the sealed windows and air-conditioning insulated the travellers from the outside world. So, while enthusiasts clicked stop-watches to prove that the train really was running at 125, business travellers worked, grandparents read and children played, all unaware that they were travelling at over two miles a minute.

In spite of the success of the IC125s, however, there was more disappointing news on the horizon when it came to the size of the HST fleet itself. Originally, InterCity had planned a production programme which would see a 161 strong fleet of IC125s operating on all the non-electrified main lines. These sets would cover services on the East Coast main line, on the West of England services from Paddington, on the Cross Country services from the North of England and Scotland to the South West as well as a number of secondary InterCity routes such as Edinburgh-Glasgow and the Trans-Pennine route. But it was not to be. By the time that the Western Region's services had started, Britain was falling into recession and British Rail was having to fight to justify investment in every new train.

East Coast expectations

When the East Coast inaugurated its new high speed services in May 1978 there were not enough InterCity 125s for the full timetable due to delays in their delivery. Instead a hybrid service with additional locomotive-hauled trains was provided. Once again the 'nose cone effect' was demonstrated. Passengers were willing to stand to get the speed and comfort advantages of the InterCity 125 while there were seats to spare in the slower stand to get the speed and comfort advantages of the InterCity 125 while there were seats to spare in the slower locomotive-hauled trains.

Improvement to and renewal of the infrastructure is a continuous process; mostly carried out at night and during weekends, this typical scene is on the approaches to York Station

Then, just as the East Coast main line was preparing for the full launch of its Anglo-Scottish InterCity 125 services in May 1979, tragedy struck as a tunnel collapsed at Penmanshiel in Scotland killing two workers. It was, therefore, not until August 1979 that the full InterCity 125 services were introduced.

Improvements on track

On the East Coast too, the role of the civil engineers was vital in making sustained, high speed cruising possible. They had been driven since the 1960s by the commercial need to reduce journey times on a route with severe air and motorway competition and they had worked relentlessly to save precious minutes. They developed an incremental programme of improvements which simplified the authorisation of funding compared to a total route upgrading scheme. Improvements were worked up which saved two minutes here and three minutes there. For example, in 1967 line speed improvements gave a benefit of some 15 minutes between London and Newcastle for a total expenditure of just £750,000.

Even better, the cumulative effect of journey time savings made each scheme more affordable than the last. As an example, in 1969, it became feasible to realign curves at Offord in Cambridgeshire to raise the speed limit from 70 mph to 100 mph even though this work meant encroaching upon and diverting the course of the River

Ouse. As a result of all of these small but vital improvements, at the start of the 1970 timetable a line speed of 95/100 mph was available for some 160 out of the 268 miles between London and Newcastle. The figure just three years earlier had been a mere 77 miles.

These steady steps to success paved the way for even more ambitious schemes which saw the remodelling of Peterborough station where line speed through the station itself was raised from 20 to 105 mph. In addition, other major improvements were also carried out at Hatfield, Grantham, Selby and between Darlington and Newcastle.

The first trains to exploit this engineering work were the famous 'Deltic plus eight' formations. These trains, limited to eight coaches with a 3,300 hp diesel-electric at the head end, brought journey times down dramatically in advance of the introduction of InterCity 125s. When the Deltics were launched in 1962 they introduced a 6 hour London to Edinburgh timing. By the time that they handed over to IC125s, this had been cut to 5 hours 27 minutes.

Transport economists have calculated that it is journey time and not distance that is the critical factor in the competition between rail and air, there being a changeover point from one mode to the other around the three hours' mark. On the East Coast, IC125 made London to Newcastle a three hour journey, nearly one hour being slashed off the best Deltic timing. This was achieved through the East Coast's relentless strategy of route improvements and no less than 260 of the 393 miles on the London to Edinburgh journey were being run at 100 mph and above by the end of the 1970s.

Peterborough Station before rebuilding - all passenger trains had to take the same path through the station, and were subject to a 20 mph speed limit. The lines to the right were sidings and freight lines

Peterborough Station after rebuilding - the freight lines were reconstructed for 105 mph running and new platforms built, so that express trains could by-pass stopping services

Winning in the West of England

Meanwhile, the Government had authorised a further 14 sets for the Western Region for operation of its West of England services to Somerset, Devon and Cornwall. That the investment case could be made for a line with hardly any track cleared for more than 110 mph west of Reading demonstrated yet another of the strengths of IC125: even when the sets were unable to run at their full design speed, the superior acceleration and braking characteristics could bring valuable time savings whilst the improved ambience would also attract passengers. A partial West Country service was introduced in October 1979, with the full IC125 timetable starting in May 1980.

The HST's ability to save time without needing to exploit its 125 mph potential was one of the key reasons for the InterCity 125 being so attractive to the State Rail Authority of New South Wales in Australia. Re-geared for 100 mph, acceleration was even better and InterCity XPT was able to transform journeys which had previously required an overnight stop into straightforward day returns.

Cross Country goes HST

Back in the UK, however, and despite InterCity 125's commercial success, investment was getting increasingly difficult to obtain. InterCity sought authority in 1978 to add a further 36 trains to its North East/South West services better known today as the Cross Country business.

Implementation was planned in two stages. An initial batch of 18 trains would provide services from Edinburgh, Newcastle and Leeds to Cardiff, Bristol, Plymouth and Penzance. A second tranche would extend IC125 to services between the North West and South West and South Coast destinations. However, with nationalised industry investment under severe pressure and InterCity ridership also suffering from the recession, approval for the first batch was finally obtained in 1978 with the planned second stage being abandoned.

East Coast overcrowding

Meanwhile, the success of IC125 on the East Coast was causing severe overcrowding, highlighting the short-sighted decision to cut back the original submission for 42 trains sets. In response, InterCity put forward a submission for a further seven IC125s. These would be used to give Sheffield a peak hour service to and from King's Cross and would add Middlesbrough and Hull to the high speed network as well as beefing-up midday Anglo-Scottish services.

When the Department of Transport said that it could justify only two sets, a public storm erupted over what became known as the 'two for seven' affair. With BR's frustrated aspirations made public for once, the Department was forced to reconsider and four trains were eventually authorised in January 1980. These sets brought

HST technology for export – Australia's version, originally called InterCity XPT

Its experimental work completed, the APT-E after acceptance by the National Railway Museum, York

the total number of IC125s ordered to 95 and marked the end of production. From then on there were never to be enough of these superb trains and the shortage became particularly clear when the re-organisation of BR into business sectors in 1982 resulted in a widescale reallocation of the fleet onto the most profitable routes.

An unfulfilled promise

In contrast, the Advanced Passenger Train never overcame the year-long boycotting by the unions which meant that it was always in the shadow of the increasingly commercially successful IC125. Yet, when APT-E began running it soon demonstrated the potential of tilting trains. Sadly, in the late 1980s, this capability was to be exploited commercially elsewhere by ABB of Sweden and by FIAT of Italy. Nevertheless, in trial running APT-E demonstrated the speed potential for a tilting train to clip journey times on curving routes before it was eventually consigned to the National Railway Museum at York. In August 1975 the high speed test programme was completed in spectacular style with a number of runs on the Western Region between Swindon and Reading. On the final run the four car train maintained 152 mph for a distance of six miles.

More significant in many ways was the run between London and Leicester in October the same year when the twisting 99 miles were covered in 58 minutes at an average speed of 102.4 mph. The line speed was raised from 110 mph to 125 mph for this run with a burst of 135 mph allowed between Luton and Bedford. The notorious Market Harborough curve, then a 50 mph

restriction, was taken at 75 mph. It is interesting to contrast this future potential with the 1993 schedule for the IC125 Pullman running non-stop south from Leicester which took 71 minutes with the line speed still limited to 110 mph.

According to the original programme, APT-E was to have been followed by four pre-series trains designated APT-P. With InterCity 125 already being ordered for the non-electrified routes and the gas-turbine power plants of APT-E having failed to meet expectations, the pre-series trains were destined for the Euston to Glasgow route which was due to be fully electrified in 1974.

But the APT programme was already slipping. The original 1968 prospectus had planned to have the pre-series trains in service in 1974. Instead, they were not even ordered until that year and the quantity was cut back from four to three. It was now the intention to get them into service in 1977 with a London to Glasgow timing of four hours offering an average of just over 100 mph.

To achieve this, each train had two 4000 hp power cars marshalled between two rakes of six articulated trailer cars. This formation was put forward because only one pantograph could be used at any one time to avoid creating a bounce in the contact wire. BR was not allowed to run a high voltage cable along the train to provide a power car at each end despite the use of this solution on the French TGV fleet. This meant duplicating catering and other facilities in the rakes of coaches on either side of the power cars as passengers were not allowed to pass through these. Not surprisingly, such a formation could not have been used economically in commercial service.

APT-P spawned a number of innovations, possibly the most significant of which was the use of long, extruded aluminium sections welded together to produce the coach bodies. British Rail pioneered this 'plank' production method with the Swiss firm Alusuisse on the APT-P. It was subsequently to transform the use of aluminium in rail vehicle construction world-wide and was employed in Britain in multiple unit trains such as Regional Railways Class 158 and the family of Networker trains.

Technical innovations

Another innovation was the hydrokinetic brake. With a maximum speed of 155 mph, it was considered that APT-P needed to go beyond the friction disc brake used in InterCity 125. Instead of discs, the passenger vehicles had tubular axles inside which were small water turbines. To apply the brakes, fluid was allowed into the axle and the churning action of the turbine blades slowed the train.

Although tilting had been proved to work on APT-E, a new design of tilt mechanism was developed and this was providing a greatly improved response. So good a response, in fact, that it was easy to be fooled into believing that the train was still upright. However, in spite of these many clear technological benefits APT-P struggled, partly because of a mid-project re-organisation when APT was transferred from the Research Division to the Mechanical & Electrical Engineering Department and partly because the project continually lived in the shadow of the IC125 which continued to go from strength to strength.

The first APT power car did not roll out until mid 1977. One year later, the first three trailer cars were ceremonially unveiled but it was not until 1979 that the first test train started running with two power cars and six trailers. Nonetheless, progress was encouraging once testing started. So much so that it culminated in a new United Kingdom speed record of 160 mph between Quintinshill and Beattock on the West Coast main line on 20th December 1979. As a result, there was well-grounded confidence that APT, running at 125 mph, would start revenue earning service between London and Glasgow with the introduction of the May 1980 timetable.

It was not to be. On 18th April 1980, during a high speed proving run, the bolts holding one of the hollow axles together failed and the train derailed at 125 mph with the British Rail Vice-Chairman on board. Happily, no-one was hurt but the project never seemed to recover from this blow. Despite the APT being central to the future of the West Coast route, the project never received the resourcing needed to make it an early success.

Following APT-P, Inter-City planned to acquire a fleet of 60 trains for the West Coast, with the first being delivered in 1983 and with timetabled services starting in

The pre-production APT leans into the curves on the West Coast main line

*The pre-production APT negotiates the curvaceous
West Coast route*

1984. However, the service entry date slipped continuously. In the end APT-P made its first run in revenue earning service between Glasgow and London on 7th December 1981. Leaving Glasgow Central at 0700, it arrived one minute early at Euston at 1115. It had averaged 102 mph between Preston and London and had reached a top speed of 137 mph. This run was hailed as the beginning of success but two subsequent runs were dogged with problems, from freezing brake pipes to a chafing wire and to tilt failure. Service running was abandoned after just one week.

West Coast options

In 1982, sectorisation had been introduced and InterCity became a business in its own right. The APT programme was then put under very close scrutiny. The unavoidable conclusion was that APT was no longer what the business needed and high speed, locomotive-hauled options began to be considered for the West Coast route.

During 1982, trial running restarted with APT-P carrying railway staff and their families to test on board systems. At the same time, however, the London Midland Region team was actively investigating the possibility of converting HSTs to electric traction for that route. This too was to be a lost opportunity and, in one last throw, John Mitchell, one of the original members of the Research Division's team which created the APT concept, was appointed APT Project Manager and more engineers were drafted into the development team.

The APT was made to work reliably in just a few months but already the future of the project was looking less than promising. In 1983, the train was withdrawn once more as the bolts in the hollow axles again proved troublesome. Meanwhile, the design of the APT had evolved through an alphabet of variants until APT-U was proposed with tilting coaches marshalled with a non-tilting power car with driving cab. Gone was articulation, to be replaced by conventional bogies. Gone was the hydrokinetic brake, now to be replaced with discs. This concept then evolved into IC225, of which more later, which was adopted as a common design for both the West Coast and for the East Coast main line electrifications.

By the time IC225 went out to tender for the East Coast electrification, the power car had become the Class 91 locomotive, an entirely new design by GEC Alsthom. Similarly, the lightweight aluminium vehicles had become the steel-bodied Mark IV coach. The only hint of the original dream were the tapered sides of the Mark IV body, which would allow it to tilt – that is if fitting tilting equipment could ever be justified.

And that was the end of APT which, nonetheless, saved its best for last. On 12th December 1984, there was a tantalising reminder of what might have been with a run from Euston to Glasgow in 3 hours 52 minutes 45 sec. It was not enough to save the project, unfortunately, and one train was preserved in 1986 with the remainder of the vehicles sold for scrap. By then the Class 91 had been ordered. Significantly, key posts on that project were held by former APT engineers who had left BR as they saw the original vision fail. This time, they were determined to get it right and from the moment it rolled out on schedule on St Valentine's Day 1988, the Class 91 has proved to be the real success that APT could have been.

An electric locomotive - hauled train on the northern section of the West Coast main line in Cumbria

Weaver to Glasgow electrification

On the darker side, the failure of the APT was to handicap the West Coast main line for the rest of the century. In 1970, the Government had authorised the extension of the 1966 London to Liverpool/Manchester electrification northwards from Weaver Junction, via Preston, Lancaster and Carlisle to Glasgow. That further electrification, authorised at a time when the railway's finances were under severe pressure, was, in large part due to the success of the original sixties' scheme.

Those new services to and from Manchester and Liverpool were inaugurated in 1966 and by 1970 this intensive electric service had doubled ridership on the route, had given InterCity a 40% share of the market and forced competing airline operators to cut back their schedules, thus presaging the opening of the TGV between Paris and Lyons some two decades later. Completed in the spring of 1974, the Crewe to Glasgow electrification repeated the earlier success story as the "sparks effect" again caught the travelling public's imagination. Overnight, the northern fells were tamed. Where trains had required double heading with diesel locomotives to achieve acceptable times over the difficult climbs of Shap and Beattock, the new 5,000 hp Class 87 electric locomotives stormed up these gradients at line speed. At the same time, the route received its first locomotive-hauled Mark III coaches and, from the customer's

viewpoint, the West Coast main line had achieved its total route modernisation. One result was a five hour timing for the London to Glasgow 'Royal Scot', half an hour faster than the then best time of the Deltics on the East Coast. Day trips between Euston and Glasgow were offered to popularise the memorable new service.

"Sparks effect" again

By the autumn of 1974, passenger traffic on the West Coast line, the former London & North Western Railway's 'Premier Route', was already up by over 50% on the previous year. In 1978 there were 165 runs in the West Coast timetable averaging 80 mph or more but, by that time, the rival East Coast was preparing to launch its Anglo-Scottish IC125 service with a 4 hour 37 minutes timing. Had the APT programme proceeded to plan, the West Coast route would have seen its next step forward with a four hour London to Glasgow timing at the end of the 1980s to challenge the air market. Instead, the route remained trapped in the mid 1970s timetable whilst south of Crewe, infrastructure laid in the 1960s began to deteriorate from years of hammering under the intensive locomotive-hauled services.

Hard times ahead

We have seen how the introduction of HSTs on the Great Western and East Coast main lines had revolutionised travel. On other routes, however, there was a very different picture. Elderly Mark II coaches and even more elderly Mark I stock dating from the early 1960s continued to be hauled by ageing diesel locomotives on such major arteries as the Midland main line from St Pancras to Nottingham and Sheffield, on the Great Eastern between Liverpool Street and Norwich and on the cross-country link between the North East and South West England. In all, services with traction and trains not designed to give the most positive image for InterCity.

Nor were prospects for improvement good. The 1970s were coming to a close during the country's regularly-occurring economic recessions and the Labour Government announced in a 1977 White Paper on Transport Policy that InterCity services "must aim to make their full contribution to the cost of providing the infrastructure, if they are to justify continuing investment in this development".

Politicians demand profits

It was no surprise that the new Conservative Government continued this commercial policy for InterCity. On 17th March 1980 the Conservatives announced new interim targets for the InterCity business which had been agreed with the Board and which were clearly intended to concentrate InterCity minds. ✈

The 1980s saw the emphasis move from technical hardware towards customer service

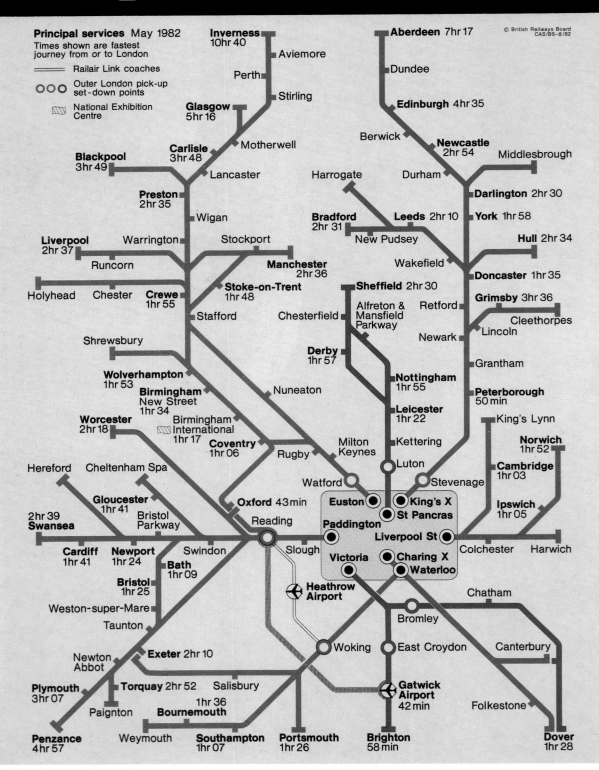

Inter-City Services

© British Railways Board
CAS/BS-8/82

Principal services May 1982
Times shown are fastest
journey from or to London

===== Railair Link coaches

○○○ Outer London pick-up
set-down points

◸ National Exhibition
Centre

Inverness 10hr 40
Aviemore
Perth
Stirling
Glasgow 5hr 16
Motherwell
Carlisle 3hr 48
Lancaster
Blackpool 3hr 49
Preston 2hr 35
Wigan
Liverpool 2hr 37
Warrington
Stockport
Runcorn
Manchester 2hr 36
Stoke-on-Trent 1hr 48
Holyhead Chester Crewe 1hr 55
Stafford
Shrewsbury
Wolverhampton 1hr 53
Birmingham New Street 1hr 34
Worcester 2hr 18
Birmingham International 1hr 17
Coventry 1hr 06
Rugby
Nuneaton
Hereford Cheltenham Spa
Gloucester 1hr 41
Bristol Parkway
2hr 39 Swansea
Cardiff 1hr 41
Newport 1hr 24
Swindon
Bath 1hr 09
Bristol 1hr 25
Weston-super-Mare
Taunton
Newton Abbot
Exeter 2hr 10
Salisbury
Plymouth 3hr 07
Torquay 2hr 52
1hr 36
Bournemouth
Paignton
Penzance 4hr 57
Weymouth
Southampton 1hr 07
Portsmouth 1hr 26

Aberdeen 7hr 17
Dundee
Edinburgh 4hr 35
Berwick
Newcastle 2hr 54
Middlesbrough
Harrogate Durham
Darlington 2hr 30
Bradford 2hr 31
Leeds 2hr 10
York 1hr 58
New Pudsey
Hull 2hr 34
Wakefield
Doncaster 1hr 35
Sheffield 2hr 30
Grimsby 3hr 36
Alfreton & Mansfield Parkway
Retford
Chesterfield
Cleethorpes
Newark
Lincoln
Derby 1hr 57
Grantham
Nottingham 1hr 55
Peterborough 50 min
Leicester 1hr 22
King's Lynn
Kettering
Norwich 1hr 52
Milton Keynes
Cambridge 1hr 03
Luton
Watford
Stevenage
Oxford 43 min
Euston
King's X
St Pancras
Reading
Paddington
Liverpool St
Ipswich 1hr 05
Slough
Victoria
Charing X
Waterloo
Colchester Harwich
Heathrow Airport
Chatham
Bromley
Woking
East Croydon
Canterbury
Gatwick Airport 42 min
Folkestone
Brighton 58 min
Dover 1hr 28

The 'Overground' map of 1982

34

Chapter Three

PUSHING FOR PROFIT ~
1982~1993

The Swallow logo symbolised the InterCity success story

The 1982 to 1993 era was one of dramatic change and growth within InterCity. It saw the business come of age and become an independent, profitable sector competing successfully with deregulated coach and air services and with its strongest competitor – the private motor car.

InterCity's progress in the 1980s and 1990s makes an interesting business case study. The change in InterCity's strategic direction linked with a focused attack on basic costs helped to provide the foundation stones for success. The main theme running through the 1980s was the push for profit. It began as a desire to differentiate InterCity as the commercial arm of British Rail. It culminated in a major financial turnround which delivered a profit for six consecutive years. The means of this achievement were to be found in business sectorisation and in the emphasis on productivity, marketing initiatives, redefinitions of the InterCity portfolio and strategic investment. This chapter will place these ingredients in their historical context up to its achievement of full business brand status in 1993.

Organising for InterCity

1982 saw the transformation of InterCity into a business sector under a new, much more accountable set of management arrangements. This provided the catalyst for change throughout the rest of the decade. On 4th January 1982 BR was split into five independent but inter-related sectors, each with bottom-line responsibility for control over costs and revenue, even if that resulted at times in difficult and complicated working relationships. It had to become a business with a clear and closely identifiable commercial role.

Deregulated road coaches concentrated the InterCity mind to meet the competition

One of the "five fingers of the late Sir Robert Reid's controlling hand" under the new sectorisation arrangements and the person appointed to meet InterCity's difficult and somewhat ambitious target of breaking even by 1985, was Cyril Bleasdale, the former managing director of Freightliners Limited. The InterCity network was clearly defined in 1982 and was intended to include all the profitable main lines including:

- The East Coast between Kings Cross and Edinburgh with trains penetrating through as far as Aberdeen.
- The West Coast between Euston and Glasgow with sleeper trains penetrating into the Highlands.
- The Great Western between Paddington, Bristol, South Wales and the West Country route to Plymouth with penetrating services through to Penzance.
- The Midland between St Pancras, Derby, Nottingham and Sheffield
- The Cross Country services between North West and North East England and South Wales, the South West of England and the South Coast.

Productivity InterCity style

To operate InterCity's 2000 mile network the business used 3400 passenger vehicles and 362 locomotives. Under sectorisation, one team could take an overall view of the needs and resources of the InterCity network for the first time and could re-allocate assets and stock to meet the changing needs of customers. Within ten years InterCity would be operating roughly the same services with 33% less rolling stock.

HSTs had first been introduced with a generous allocation of new stock on the Western Region. By May 1980 all principal trains on the Region, including services on the West of England line were HSTs. Completion of the M4 motorway paralleling the Great Western main lines to Bristol and South Wales soon attracted low-cost coach competition and this led to a significant fall in rail traffic in the early 1980s. One of the advantages of sectorisation in its early days was the development of a national business strategy which overcame the old regional parochialism. The reallocation of seven HSTs from the Western to the Midland main line in October 1982 was a classic example of a national InterCity decision which improved net profit for the business.

Up until this time, the Midland main line between St Pancras, Sheffield, Derby and Nottingham had been treated as something of a poor relation when it came to allocating modern rolling stock to the route. Trains were powered by elderly Class 45 diesel locomotives, limited to 90 mph, and formed of Mark II coaches offering journey times that fell far below standards on other InterCity main lines.

The image of the Midland was transformed when five HST units were cascaded from the Western Region at the beginning of the October 1982 timetable, to be joined by a further two units from the East Coast and three originally intended for Cross Country services. From May 1983, these sets provided the Midland with a complete HST service, save for one peak-hour train each way which continued to be locomotive-hauled. Not only had this new service been introduced by more efficient use of existing stock rather than through the provision of expensive new trains, but it had also reduced maintenance costs by ensuring that the trains formed part of a common pool of units used on both the Midland and East Coast. The cascade of HSTs to the Midland and the transformation of the its services can be seen as one of the first benefits of InterCity sector thinking.

Marketing InterCity

On 3rd October 1983 InterCity demonstrated its growing confidence by having a marketing relaunch. The most obvious sign of this to the travelling public was the decision to adopt a new and easily identifiable livery based on that formerly used on the APT. This livery was light and dark grey, separated by striking red and white bands. Internally, the re-liveried coaches – two complete sets on the Western Region and the Manchester Pullman set – received attention as InterCity experimented with new seat designs and decor to enhance the travellers' ambience. Payphones were also installed in the re-liveried units from 1984. They represented an early example of product marketing as payphones lost money but were seen as part of a larger business package. This enhanced package was aimed at attracting the First Class business traveller and included free car parking at the station, at-seat service of drinks, seat reservations on outward journey and vouchers for train meals.

A marketing setback occurred in 1983 when the Department of Transport allowed InterCity to construct no more than a third of the 180 new Mark IIIb coaches which it so badly needed to meet motorway competition. The first 32 Second Class coaches were intended to strengthen the Western Region's HST sets from a formation of two power cars plus seven coaches (2+7) to a 2+8 formation. The remaining twenty eight coaches were authorised to improve quality on the West Coast main line which had received little recent investment and where standards of both quality and speed were beginning to compare unfavourably with the rest of InterCity. From May 1984 however, maximum line speed on the West Coast was raised from 100 mph to 110 mph to exploit the new coaches and to help strengthen the investment case for the remainder.

Redefining InterCity's portfolio

A number of important UK routes nearly became part of the InterCity network in 1984. Following the Department of Transport's ruling that the InterCity business should receive no subsidy, it was invited by the Board to identify any other potentially profitable services which could fit into the InterCity portfolio. These routes included the TransPennine expresses, Edinburgh-Glasgow and Waterloo-Bournemouth. Only two routes offered the opportunity to help InterCity improve its net profitability and Liverpool Street-Norwich and Victoria-Gatwick Airport were duly transferred to InterCity in 1985.

One of the benefits of Sector overview – cascading of HSTs to the Midland main line transformed its image

It is relevant to later privatisation proposals to remember that a conflict of customer priorities had developed at Gatwick before 1984 between the needs of Southern Region commuters travelling between London and the South Coast and the demands of luggage-laden airport travellers. It was to address these differing customer needs that a dedicated 15 minute interval service called the 'Gatwick Express' was introduced at the beginning of the May 1984 timetable for those wishing to travel directly between the airport and central London.

This was a classic case of market segmentation by InterCity. Mark IId coaches were allocated to the route and refurbished, some seats being removed to provide additional luggage space. The trains were worked on a push-pull basis, power being provided by Class 73 electro-diesel locomotives. The newly transferred coaches and one locomotive (No. 73123 'Gatwick Express') were repainted in the experimental InterCity livery. Ultimately, thirteen locomotives were designated Class 73/2 and wore the same livery to emphasise their new, exclusive InterCity use.

A strategic challenge: the Serpell Report

Just as InterCity was starting to develop as a new business sector, the Serpell Report was published by the Government in January 1983. Ironically, it saw no prospect of InterCity achieving its financial target of commercial viability as set out in the 1982 Rail Plan. The Committee had been asked in May 1982 by the then Secretary of State for Transport, Mr David Howell, to: "examine within six months the finances of the railway and its associated operations, in the light of all relevant considerations, and to report on options for alternative policies and their related objectives, designed to secure improved financial results in an efficiently run railway in Great Britain over the next twenty years".

The options for change produced by the Committee could not have been more designed to destroy morale on the railways, with an Option A that identified a commercially viable system of only 1630 route miles. This option showed no railway south west of Bristol or north of Edinburgh or Glasgow. There was not even a line of railway between Newcastle and Edinburgh and the Midland main line had completely disappeared. After a bitter and protracted debate, public opinion won the day, the report was shelved, the railway network was retained and new investment was released for the start of InterCity's modernisation of the East Coast route.

East Coast Electrification

InterCity confidence in the future was materially enhanced by the announcement by the Secretary of State for Transport (the late Nicholas Ridley) on 27th July 1984 that the Government had approved a £306m scheme for the electrification of the East Coast main line northwards from Hitchin, in Hertfordshire, through to Leeds and

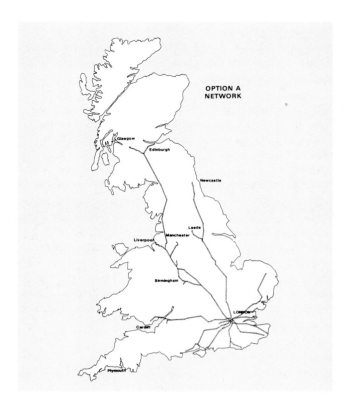

The Serpell Report recommended drastic reduction to only 1630 route miles

Edinburgh on the basis that the scheme could be funded internally through increased productivity. Of the £306m investment, just over half was attributed to infrastructure with £62m, to motive power and £74m for rolling stock. The scheme was justified primarily on savings in maintenance costs of 60% whilst reduction in journey times of around ten minutes between London and Edinburgh were also assured.

The Mayor of Durham plants the 20,000th mast of the East Coast electrification on 22nd September 1988

Planning for profit

A Board strategy document was published in December 1984. It was called 'InterCity – Into Profit' and it sought to convert an InterCity loss of £107m in 1983 into a £5m surplus by 1989. The prime agents for financial success came to be the transfer of the Anglia and Gatwick services which, once they had transferred, increased InterCity income by some £25m. An additional boost occurred in the following year when the loss-making Gloucester-Chepstow-Newport service was moved out of InterCity's remit into that of Provincial Services.

A second major contribution to profit was the identification of cost savings totalling £47m which included a seven per cent reduction in train mileage over the following five years through better tailoring of services to demand. The business also planned a 1% income growth from marketing measures such as the re-introduction of Pullman services. The re-launch of the 'Tees-Tyne Pullman' was carried out in style on 27th September 1985 when an HST made a special run from Newcastle to London in 2 hours 9 minutes at an average speed of 115 mph.

It is difficult to imagine now just how daunting was the task that InterCity faced in the mid 1980s in its quest to achieve profitability. Nevertheless, there was some good news. The Western Region had been worst hit by the drop in passenger traffic as a result of motorway competition but the loss was arrested in 1984 and was followed by a very welcome surge in demand. Loadings in 1985 averaged about ten per cent above those of the previous winter, helped by bad weather, bad road conditions and a coach strike in South Wales. At least five per cent of this traffic was believed to have been new business.

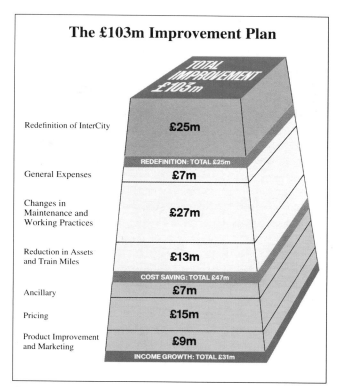

The £103m Improvement Plan

Source: InterCity – Into Profit, December 1984

A Special Train, composed of InterCity liveried coaches, offers its clients unparalleled Highland views

Marketing in the boom

The non-stop Gatwick Express service was an immediate success. It took only 30 minutes, but a long layover at the end of each journey was built into the timetable so that a train was always available for boarding. A trolley service was provided from the outset and the format proved highly successful. This provided the model and inspiration for the 'InterCity Shuttle' services introduced on other routes in the 1990s. Passenger numbers on Gatwick Express increased by 38% in the first year of operation and revenue shot up by some 52%. By the 1990s rail had a quarter of all passenger travel to and from Gatwick Airport.

The mid-1980s also saw the beginning of long-distance commuting on a grand scale as people began to realise that they could travel daily to London by HST from Didcot, Swindon or even Bath and Bristol in far less time than was required for many shorter journeys on Network SouthEast's electric system from Surrey, Sussex and Kent. Journeys between Bristol and Paddington increased by no less than 20% in the 1986 boom. Season ticket price increases well in excess of the rate of inflation were being applied by the end of the 1980s but a fifteen minute interval service was still required between Swindon and Paddington to meet peak demands. Commuters now accounted for some ten per cent of InterCity Great Western's income and that income helped to make it the first InterCity route to move into profit. The electrification of the East Coast at the end of the decade enabled additional HSTs to be returned to Great Western in order to meet this growing commuter demand and enabled all GW HSTs to be reformed into 2+8 sets to provide additional seats.

Financial performance 1987-88

John Prideaux took over InterCity in February 1986. He focused on the need for major cost reductions. The Government target remained a 2.7% return on net assets and the Annual Report for 1987/88 recorded an encouraging 19% reduction in InterCity's operating loss together with a 5% increase in passenger volume. This impressive performance had been helped by a series of highly focused business activities. Refurbishment of the InterCity fleet brought a dramatic change in perception amongst customers. At the same time a more sophisticated approach to marketing was taken which involved streamlining products and restructuring the ticket range in order to optimise revenue per seat. The expansion of the Pullman network in 1987 helped to enhance product quality and to expand the First Class business market. New Pullman services were introduced including 'The Master Cutler', 'The Golden Hind' and the 'Birmingham Pullman'. All of these had helped to contribute towards a 15% increase in First Class ticket sales.

Gatwick Express – prototype for InterCity Shuttle services. This view shows the dedicated platform at Victoria

*Silver Standard offers enhanced service to holders of full fare
Standard tickets*

Improved quality was introduced between Liverpool
and Euston with the introduction of Silver Standard
service. This provided specially identified accommodation
with free seat reservations and with an at-seat service
of complimentary light refreshments to passengers
holding full fare Standard tickets. One of the best
achievements of InterCity in the late 1980s was
maintaining its timetable of frequent, regular-interval
services thoughout the recession.

Profit at last: 1988-89

The BRB's Annual Report for 1988/89 proudly
announced that "in its first year as a fully commercial
business, InterCity turned an operating loss of £86m into a
profit of £57m. Income rose by 10% and traffic volume
rose by 4% to record levels.

The transfer of routes, the economic boom and a
maintenance 'holiday' had all helped to deliver a profit.
Electrification had reached Norwich by May 1987 and the
results had been good. Both fleet and infrastructure
made considerable contributions to the 1987/88 financial
achievement. Substantial reductions in rolling stock unit
costs were achieved by rationalising heavy maintenance
work at key strategic depots, whilst an intense review of
maintenance schedules led to cost savings of £15m. A
review of infrastructure working practices in the late
1980s looked specifically at weekend engineering work
and helped to lower the cost of track maintenance. The
infrastructure cost initiative reaped major savings for the

business but could never be a substitute for the economies
that would flow from investment in major route
modernisation.

West Coast interim strategy

In contrast with other InterCity routes, the West Coast
main line had made little progress for a number of years.
The failure of the APT experiment in the mid 1980s had
left this important main line struggling with equipment
which the tilting train had been designed to replace. By
1987 InterCity had recognised that its strength lay in
competing for journeys of up to three hours in duration
and had shifted its emphasis from the historically
important Euston to Glasgow line to the more profitable
routes from London to the West Midlands, Liverpool and
Manchester, where the last deliveries of Mark III coaching
stock had been introduced in 1987 to create an all air-
conditioned service.

In the following year, the West Coast received some
welcome new equipment intended to enhance efficiency
and productivity. Driving Van Trailers (or DVTs) –
designed to save locomotives by creating self-contained
train sets – began to be delivered to the route. Fifty two
were ordered to work with new Class 90 locomotives,
whilst existing Class 86 and 87 locomotives were
converted to enable push-pull working to be introduced.
The first 110mph Class 90 was delivered towards the end
of 1987. There was some disappointment that 125 mph
locomotives had not been specified but, nonetheless, the
new arrivals did mean that some increasingly troublesome
older locomotives from the 1960s could be withdrawn.
The new Class 90s and their DVTs improved reliability

East Coast electrification brought the best-ever service to the London – North East England – Scotland route

and efficiency on the West Coast even though there were some initial teething problems with the DVTs themselves. These rolling stock improvements bought time for the West Coast before the infrastructure fell due for renewal in the 1990s.

East Coast electrification commissioned

In the meantime, full electrification and other modernisation of the East Coast route took place between 1984 and 1991. In the same timescale the InterCity 225 train was developed, brought into production and introduced into full service. The IC225 consisted of the powerful new Class 91 electric locomotive and its stylish Mark IV coaches. The first Class 91 locomotive was rolled out at Crewe on 14th February 1988 and commenced its intensive running-in period.

Electric haulage of some services between Kings Cross and Leeds began in August of that year, using the experimental Brush Traction locomotive No. 89001 and Mark III coaches. The Leeds electrification was not only finished ahead of schedule but worked out at approximately half the cost of the pioneering West Coast project twenty years earlier after allowance for inflation.

Class 91s began revenue earning service on 3rd March 1989, and from the beginning of that summer's timetable five train diagrams were scheduled for haulage by these new locomotives. Their speed as well as their power was ably demonstrated later in the year when new Mark IV coaches and No. 91001 'Swallow' were involved in high

speed tests between Grantham and Peterborough, during which a top speed of 162.2mph was reached.

The thirty one new East Coast trains were known as InterCity 225s to reflect their top design speed of 225km/h (140mph). In practice, the line speed remained limited to 200km/h (125mph) and there is little prospect of this changing until significant investment can be found – particularly for upgrading signalling in many areas. The first complete IC225 train – Class 91 and Mark IV coaches – to enter passenger service did so on 2nd October 1989 on the Leeds-London 'Yorkshire Pullman'. As deliveries proceeded apace further InterCity 225 formations were introduced regularly. On 14th May 1990, with the summer timetable, the full IC225 service to Leeds was introduced.

Wiring of the short stretch of railway from Carstairs to Edinburgh was planned as part of the Weaver Junction to Glasgow electrification back in the 1970s. It was finally sponsored by Cross Country – to eliminate diesel-haulage of trains between Edinburgh and West Coast destinations – but it also enabled East Coast IC225s to be extended to Glasgow allowing a much more attractive through service between that city and the North East of England and Yorkshire.

With electrification in place and completion of the Newcastle resignalling, IC225 services to Scotland began in mid-1991 and the largest, single modernisation scheme ever to be undertaken on Britain's railways was completed. The whole package brought the best ever service between London, Yorkshire, North East England and Central Scotland and was based on hard, commercial planning.

InterCity becomes a business

In 1990 InterCity was still a small commercial organisation with a relatively small staff of its own – some 3,000 together with a further 2,400 in On Board Services. InterCity was required to provide passenger services over the main lines linking Britain's principal cities without any contribution from Government grant. The business was dependent on six geographical Regions with very different histories and business cultures for the actual delivery of the product it marketed. They provided lines, stations and rolling stock.

A successful new organisation, 'Organising for Quality', was implemented in shadow form in 1991. This united the General Managers of the former Regions as Directors of the five new InterCity routes. An InterCity Directors' Group was established and this was given the task of fully integrating the five InterCity routes into one, forward-looking profitable business.

In April 1991 the East Coast route, the Great Western and the Anglia/Gatwick operation were fully absorbed into the new organisation and in April 1992 the dissolution of the London Midland Region allowed the final InterCity to emerge. It brought the providers of the services into one organisation and equipped them with all the assets needed to work and market those services. A real railway company was created; a company which owned its assets and employed its own staff. In addition, it managed its own £1 billion balance sheet under the control of a new Finance Director from Trust House Forte, Geoff Ashton. For the first time since 1948 a genuine railway business had been put together in a form the outside world could recognise.

Chris Green was appointed Managing Director in January 1992 with the remit to commission the new organisation from April and to maintain profitability despite the deepening economic recession. Radical changes would be needed in both the cost structures and the marketing of InterCity to deliver these targets and it was quickly recognised that a major shift would be needed in the company's culture. Such changes could not happen without much careful planning and great goodwill.

The new organisation set up specific levels of responsibility between the InterCity business headquarters and the five route headquarters. InterCity headquarters dealt with strategic planning, marketing and finance including the development of a strong national brand. In addition, considerable time and effort were devoted to training and development to create a proactive business culture. Inter-City's Infrastructure Director, John Elliott, ensured that a significant proportion of the savings the civil engineers contributed to the improvement of InterCity finances was re-invested. Revolutionary track renewal equipment was purchased to help them in their quest for higher productivity with minimal impact on the service to the customer.

What was put in place between 1990 and 1992 was, without doubt, the best organisation that British Rail ever had, the tragedy was that Organising for Quality came too

From 1992, InterCity owned its assets including maintenance machinery – such as this revolutionary High-Output Ballast Cleaner

Cross Country strategy – specially adapted Class 47/8 locomotives met the market with shorter trains

late. For InterCity, it brought a very sharp focus to the railway, uniting a family of 30,000 staff in the common purpose of achieving the InterCity vision.

Cross Country strategy

InterCity was convinced of the positive merits of its HSTs and it put considerable energy into examining the case for forming half-HSTs to work on Cross Country services. However, not only would the cost of this solution have been too high, but there would have been an unbridgeable time-gap in which units were out of service. A study was made of the costs and benefits of running HSTs 'under the wires' to Aberdeen and other places off electrified routes. A similar study led to the introduction of HSTs on Euston-Holyhead services in 1991 which ran 'under the wires' from London to Crewe.

If there could be no half-HSTs, what was to be done for Cross Country? The answer was the short-train solution, with Class 47-hauled formations of Mark IIf vehicles able to run close to HST timings, which were limited on these routes. There was a problem with the elderly locomotives which had been designed for a maximum speed of 95 mph, but which had become used to working at significantly lower speeds. Approaching the end of their lives, they were now being required to run at their maximum speed for long distances. A number of them were subsequently equipped with larger fuel tanks and bigger brake blocks and were concentrated on Bristol Bath Road depot for maintenance. The modifications and allocation to one depot all helped to deliver the product. What did not help was the conclusion that the clasp brakes

of the Mark IIf vehicles were not predictable enough in their performance to allow lightweight five coach trains to be worked at 95 mph so that eventually an increase of the formation to seven vehicles was required.

Maximising the InterCity fleet

Completion of the East Coast project allowed a huge shake-out of stock to take place, leaving a fleet properly reflecting the quality railway that the InterCity vision sought. Essentially, nothing earlier than Mark IIf remained and what was left was refurbished to a consistently high standard. The East Coast and the Great Western became 125 mph railways and the Midland and the West Coast became 110 mph railways with the latter being rationalised to three train types. Anglia operated at 100 mph with Mark IIf vehicles, and Cross Country became a 125/Class 47 short-train railway operating at 95/100 mph. No less than two thirds of the core fleet was made up of Mark III vehicles built between 1974 and 1984. Such a chain of events demonstrated the strength of a national InterCity organisation able to survey its entire operation and deploy its fleet to the best advantage of the whole business and to the benefit of the greatest number of customers.

During the early 1990s InterCity also learnt to prioritise its markets. Rather than offering a token train service to a wide number of destinations it contracted its resources to ensure excellence on its core routes. This resulted in the scrapping of much second-rate rolling stock and the strengthening of primary services. InterCity's withdrawal from Shrewsbury and Blackpool in 1992 and Cleethorpes in 1993 enabled InterCity to make significant savings and also allowed the Great Western to withdraw all its locomotive-hauled passenger trains and provide a 100% HST operation for the first time in 1993.

The customer service revolution

The 1990s will be remembered as the era when InterCity made a major and very public commitment to the radical improvement of customer service. This was as a distinct result of extensive research into customer needs which highlighted rising consumer expectations. It made good business sense to invest in customer service at a time of intense competition.

InterCity's customer service improvements came at a time when there was a growing awareness throughout the country of consumer rights and entitlements. There was pressure to raise standards and InterCity, along with the other passenger businesses, produced the 'Passenger's Charter' in March 1992. This set targets for customer service and promised to compensate customers if the railway failed to deliver its timetable promise. In October 1993, InterCity Anglia received a prestigious customer service award when it gained the coveted 'Charter Mark' for continuous customer service improvement. This achievement helps to demonstrate how far InterCity had come from the late 1970s.

The main theme from the customer research was that over half InterCity's customers made only one or two trips a year and found rail travel stressful and unfriendly. InterCity took this finding to heart in a big way and from 1992 Customer Welcome teams appeared in their bright claret uniforms on the concourses of all the larger InterCity stations. In 1993 porters were re-introduced at King's Cross and Euston to the delight of the media and consumers alike. New Telesales services offered a freephone number for the immediate purchase of tickets using credit or debit cards. Stations were given improved directional signing, signposting, car parks were extended and new waiting rooms provided.

InterCity Shuttle

The introduction of InterCity Shuttle in May 1993 represented a culmination in the range of customer service initiatives. It brought together all these in a tangible way and presented them confidently in TV advertising. Four medium distance routes were designated Shuttle in 1993:

Route	Number of trains daily
Euston-West Midlands	56
St Pancras-East Midlands	57
Liverpool St-Norwich	32
Paddington-Bristol/South Wales	69

The total cost of Shuttle was small but the goodwill it generated was enormous and repeat business started to flow. This was particularly fortuitous since InterCity's top investment priority, the £750m West Coast modernisation, was not going well.

InterCity 250 for West Coast

The InterCity 250 project for a new West Coast train was fully approved by InterCity but was quickly stalled for funding at Board and Ministry level. This was a Total Route Modernisation project, and involved the extensive

Customer Welcome teams are at the heart of the customer service revolution

modernisation of the infrastructure, realignments for higher speed, re-electrification and the acquisition of a fleet of new trains. In 1992 InterCity wanted to buy complete trains rather than separate locomotives and coaches. This was something that had previously happened only with the HSTs – and it wanted to lay the foundations for a coherent fleet.

The aim was to get a Class 250 into service as the replacement for the obsolete Mark IIf stock and to test this thoroughly in service over a four or five year period before commissioning a high quality fleet. The new train was to be an evolution of the East Coast's InterCity 225 and could have been in service by 1995. In the summer of 1992 it finally hit the buffers for lack of funding in the depths of the recession and the tenders for the train lapsed.

Privatisation proposals precluded any further development and 1993 represented another watershed in InterCity's history. The 1980s and 1990s had been periods of great change and achievement for InterCity. The business had survived the worst post-war recession to hit the UK and had remained in profit throughout.

Profit in the recession

Despite the deepening recession, InterCity remained strongly in the black with results in 1992/93 revealing a £65m profit. This could not have been achieved without a grinding attention to attacking costs, committing the business to customer service and developing an aggressive marketing approach. InterCity Directors' Group determined in 1993 that productivity savings of 6% should be made in such a way that customers would not see any deterioration in the service offered. There was to be no change to the InterCity vision even in a financial crisis. Extensive analysis revealed what could be done. It was finally agreed to risk delegating the task down the line and to trust the staff closest to the job to deliver the savings. This was done and the results exceeded the original target.

Clearly, the strength of the new InterCity did not come from a highly-centralised organisation. With day-to-day working delegated to the lowest sensible level there was no central control point at headquarters, no central operating structure, no longer even a Director of Operations. The central management team at the business unit was there to develop policy, to think strategically and to ensure a strong voice for the routes in arguing the case for investment with Board and Government. It represented the whole InterCity business in the market place through, for example, multi-million pound television advertising initiatives which won several coveted awards and in major new ticketing initiatives such as Apex which offered road coach prices for rail speeds on selected trains.

When porters in distinctive uniforms returned to Euston and Kings Cross in 1993 they were much appreciated by customers

The use of revenue management to maximise the available ticket revenue played a vital part in marketing initiatives in the 1990s. Over long distance routes, even more competitively-priced fares such as SuperApex were introduced which effectively fought-off coach competition and helped to increase InterCity's market share. Other national marketing promotions included the reinforcement of the First Class market at a time when customers were choosing to trade down in increasing numbers from First to Standard. In addition, there were further joint leisure promotions with household names such as Boots and Shell.

The InterCity team maintained its momentum on customer service, marketing and overall productivity. The reward was a £100m profit for 1993/94; a truly exciting achievement given the economic and political conditions under which the business was working. However, the greatest frustration remained the continuing shortage of investment funding. To run a steady-state railway which renewed its assets at the right time, InterCity needed to spend £225m a year on its infrastructure and trains but in 1993-94 it only had £90m, which was barely enough to keep the railway safe and secure. No clearer example could be given of the implications that short term funding decisions can have on long term profitability than the loss of the West Coast modernisation during this period. A disappointing end to what had been an otherwise powerful and positive period for the InterCity business.

What might have been – a mock-up of Standard accommodation for InterCity 250

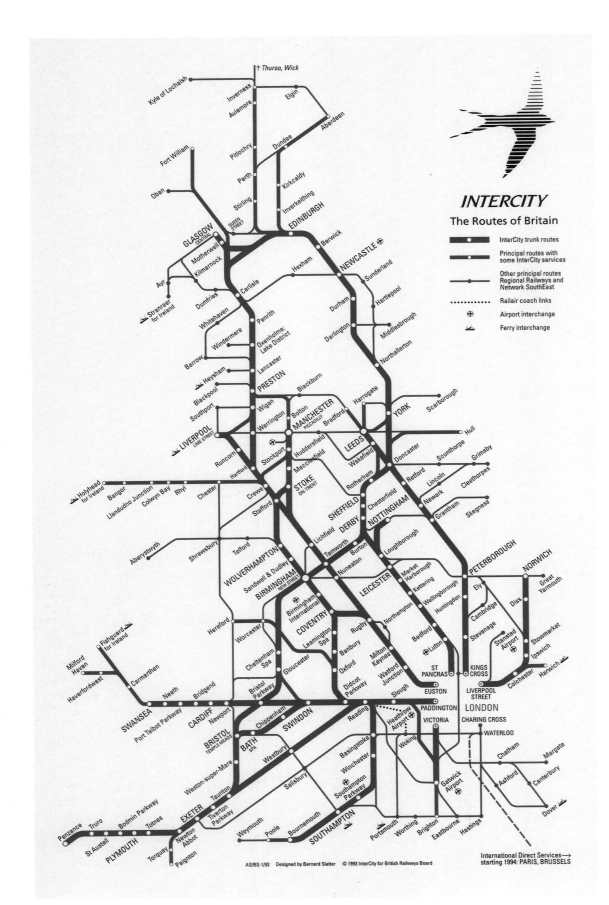

↑ Thurso, Wick

AS/BS-1/93   Designed by Bernard Slatter   © 1993 InterCity for British Railways Board

INTERCITY

The Routes of Britain

	InterCity trunk routes
	Principal routes with some InterCity services
	Other principal routes Regional Railways and Network SouthEast
	Railair coach links
⊕	Airport interchange
⚓	Ferry interchange

International Direct Services→
starting 1994: PARIS, BRUSSELS

The InterCity map in 1993 reflected a better co-ordination between the businesses with extensive inclusion of connecting services

Chapter Four

BUILDING A WINNING BRAND

The latest branding on the latest train

The story of the famous InterCity brand is a long and fascinating one which deserves a chapter to itself. InterCity as a name evokes the ideas of relaxation, comfort and fast trains speeding through the British countryside. InterCity as a business is the first profitable, national passenger railway in Europe. But InterCity is, above all, a brand with which people enjoy associating and which they choose to use again and again.

In fact, InterCity is one of the best established brand names in the United Kingdom with over ninety per cent of the population recognising the name. Its use began back in the 1960s when British Rail led branding in the travel market. Since then the InterCity business has taken the concept forward in major strides. It has passed into the

language as a general term for fast, long-distance trains – so much so that has been widely copied by railways around the world – and imitation is the sincerest form of flattery.

Successful brands

Brands are developed by marketeers to distinguish their own product from that of the competition. Marketeers in service businesses like InterCity use them to guarantee a consistent and distinctive quality of service. The customer recognises the brand, knows what to expect, chooses InterCity and hopefully goes on choosing InterCity.

Effective brands guarantee a hard functional benefit to the customer; InterCity offers fast, frequent, comfortable

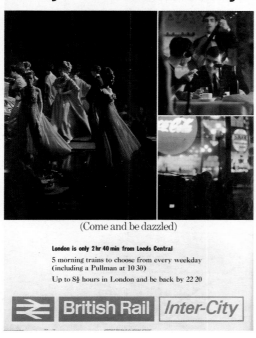

The lights of London are just a train-ride away

(Come and be dazzled)

London is only 2 hr 40 min from Leeds Central

5 morning trains to choose from every weekday (including a Pullman at 10 30)

Up to 8½ hours in London and be back by 22 20

British Rail | *Inter-City*

Leisure travel poster of 1966, one of the first promotional uses of the term Inter-City

Half-price train travel for everyone under 24.

"Now, *anyone* under the age of 24 is entitled to half-price travel with a Student Railcard – even non-students. Your Railcard will only cost you £10 – but it'll save you a lot more!

All the details are in a leaflet – pick one up at most British Rail stations."

This is the age of the train

"This is the Age of the Train" series, featuring Jimmy Savile

Business travel advertisement – 1992

A traffic jam as seen from an InterCity train.

Well. Business is all about getting ahead of the others, isn't it?

Admit it. There's something about whisking past traffic jams in an InterCity train, that appeals to your mean competitive streak.

INTERCITY

Leisure travel using Swallow logo – 1992

Leisure Travel. A guide with InterCity.

With over fifty colour pages of leisure travel ideas and information, InterCity's new Leisure Travel Guide is invaluable. You can get a copy **FREE** simply by asking at your nearest British Rail Travel Centre, or by ringing 081-200 0200

INTERCITY

Building 'brand image' through product – as exemplified in this 1988 publicity shot

trains. Really successful brands have an emotional appeal as well and a major element of InterCity's recent success has been achieved by building on the British public's emotional attachment to trains, a feeling best described as 'train magic' and an emotion particularly associated with HSTs and the InterCity business.

The use of the name Inter-City was given to a Paddington to Wolverhampton train that ran in the early 1950s. As a brand however, its origins lie in the Corporate Design Panel of 1965. The new name, British Rail, and the new logo that went with that new name, were a conscious decision to break with the past. Looking back after nearly three decades when company logos and corporate identities are the norm, it is difficult to remember just how innovative those changes were.

Breaking the mould

When electric trains began running between Euston, Manchester and Liverpool in April 1966 the improvement was so dramatic that it became known as the 'New Railway'. All the new trains on the service were called 'Inter-City' and all set new standards for speed, frequency and comfort. New television and press advertising supported the launch. Again, all emphasised the InterCity name; this was the launch of InterCity as a brand. It was also a turning point in that long-distance rail began to fight back against competition from the car, growing use of which had led to a continuous decline in train travel during the 1950s and early 1960s.

InterCity was an immediate success with customers and further television advertising, such as the Inter-City *'Heart to Heart'* campaign which was launched in 1967, built on this success. The use of the name was extended to other routes as coaches were upgraded or as new services were introduced. For example, the London to Birmingham electrification was completed in December 1967 and the new service on this line was promoted as 'Inter-City' too.

Centre to centre – 'Heart to Heart' – Early TV campaign

The marketeers always tried to ensure that the InterCity guarantee of quality meant something and that it was not just a promotional campaign or a label. This is an important principle which is the foundation of all successful brands. In September 1969, in order to enhance this guarantee, it was announced that all new InterCity coaches including Second Class were to have air-conditioning. In 1971 the first such coaches entered service. Previously, only the Blue Pullman and the

Manchester Pullman had enjoyed air conditioning. At the same time, the network was expanded away from routes based on London with the announcement that the North East/South West route from Newcastle to Bristol and Plymouth would have InterCity status.

Initiatives and innovations

Other quality improvements for the InterCity passenger included the development of Travel Centres focused on selling InterCity tickets. The partnership between the car for local journeys and the InterCity train for long distance travel was enhanced with Rail Drive car hire in 1969 and the first custom-built Parkway station at Bristol in 1972. There was a mix of success with some initiatives being less successful than others. The 'Travelling' quarterly magazine for rail passengers, for example, was relatively short-lived. On the other hand, the Executive Travel concept introduced on the East Coast between Newcastle, Bradford, Leeds and King's Cross, went on to give InterCity a long-term competitive edge.

By the mid 1970s, InterCity was well established with a modern image and a record for innovation in both product and advertising. The slogan "Inter-City makes the going easy – and the coming back" emphasised the convenience and the famous 'Monica' posters were designed to stimulate leisure travel. Further afield, overseas railways such as those in West Germany began to adopt the InterCity name in 1971.

"Monica" posters targetted the leisure traveller, in addition many fashion-conscious young women enquired as to where she bought her clothes

The distinctive nose cone quickly epitomised InterCity and all that was best in rail travel

The next major step forward in the development of InterCity came with the launch of InterCity 125 trains in 1976. These trains gave the InterCity brand whole new dimensions of speed and comfort. They also gave a much clearer visual identity to the brand with the distinctive nose cone which quickly came to signify InterCity and all that was best in rail travel. InterCity 125 was an instant success both on the Great Western and the East Coast. New advertising with the slogan "Have a good trip" stressed the benefits of speed, with the HST being known as "The Journey Shrinker".

However, the success of InterCity 125 led to BR over-reaching itself with the InterCity brand application – possibly losing some of the quality guarantee that came with it. The brand name was extended through a range of 'secondary Inter-City services' such as London to Brighton which were fairly fast but which had few of the associations with comfortable long-distance travel that had been linked with InterCity. For many this loss of direction was typified by the "This is the Age of the Train" advertising campaign intended to relaunch train travel generally. Featuring Jimmy Savile, this 1980 campaign used InterCity simply as one of the many names BR presented to the market. The distinctive InterCity identity was in danger of being lost

This loss of InterCity's focus as a brand continued as BR faced the recession of 1980/81. This bad economic news was combined in 1980 with increased competition from deregulated coaches and with the intensely difficult year of 1982 when strikes closed the railway for seventeen days. After these events, the natural reaction on the part of the railway authorities was to cut fares in order to get volume back. The Liverpool to London 'Saver' offer at £9 return did this very successfully, but the volume of traffic generated could only be carried by running extra trains. These cost money to run and, more importantly, were not generally of InterCity quality. This resulted in the whole offer merely breaking even and risked further loss of quality from the InterCity brand.

Continuing the "See a friend this weekend" theme – seven years on from Monica

"Inter-City makes the going easy" theme – 1975

Executive travel – 1980

"We're getting there" – 1985

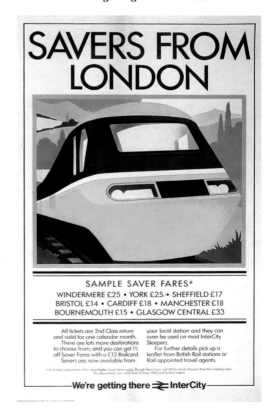

Examples of road-side advertising to attract the motorist

Birmingham to Bournemouth without changing.   *INTERCITY*

They'd notice if you drove to London at 110mph.   *INTERCITY*

Fast, off-road vehicle. With chauffeur and air con. Welcome to the train.   *INTERCITY*

Policy and people

A marketing strategy was developed that recognised that 'Inter-City' had a minor asset in the brand name, but stressed that it was vital that the name should only be used on those trains which met the quality standards associated with the brand. By definition, this killed any idea that there could be 'secondary Inter-City services'. Furthermore, the business should position itself as a quality and value-for-money operator in the travel market and should not try to compete with coach on price. InterCity should target its marketing activity more explicitly at specific segments of the market, for example, on business travellers and on leisure travellers, but should do so with the overall brand name. It was agreed that InterCity should not compete just on journey time but should be concerned with the customer's overall journey experience. Amongst other things, this would mean improving accessibility to the network as well as further developing the range and quality of customer services provided on the train.

Inter-City becomes InterCity

This strategy was put into practice over the four years 1982/86. One of the first changes to be implemented was to drop the hyphen; Inter-City became InterCity. Although this may sound a trivial step to take it began the process of creating a new and distinctive image for InterCity, now an independent business as well as a brand name. Up until this point different parts of BR had used different typefaces and had used the name InterCity in different ways. Now there was to be one clear and consistent usage and approach.

Much more significant in relation to its immediate and direct impact on the customer was the development of new services for the business traveller, culminating in the re-launch of Pullman in 1985. The business recognised that InterCity was losing out in terms of status to air as a way of travelling on business. Pullman's traditional high standards and InterCity's image of modernity redressed this balance. The leisure customer was not forgotten and the positive lessons from Savers on the Liverpool to London route were taken on board with a new range of Saver fares which was progressively extended across the country, culminating in 1985 in the introduction of a new national fares structure.

During this period further developments took place with InterCity publications. The InterCity Executive Guide (a high quality pocket timetable) was developed for the business traveller and was mailed to over 100,000 customers. It is better known today as the InterCity Guide, for all customers needing a network timetable. In 1985, the InterCity Magazine was launched for the First Class business traveller and it has become one of the most widely read publications of its type offering excellent opportunities to reinforce the brand.

Research carried out into InterCity's image in the mid-1980s suggested that some of the momentum that had

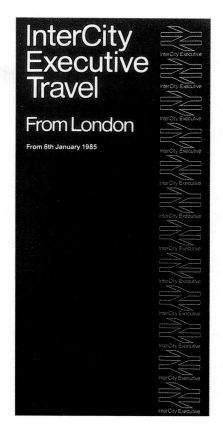

Forerunner of 'InterCity Guide to Services'

InterCity Magazine – launch poster

been generated behind the InterCity brand had not, as yet, changed public perceptions. InterCity was still seen as a name for British Rail's long distance trains but it had lost some of its distinct identity as a specific brand. This led to a review of the advertising campaign and to a demand for new commercials from new agencies. In 1984 distinctive campaigns were introduced for InterCity business travel. The still-remembered 'Plane to Train' and 'Train Jam' with their single, obvious, yet brilliantly presented messages were the most famous. They were produced by a small advertising agency which was soon taken over by Saatchi and Saatchi. This was the beginning of InterCity's long and successful relationship with Saatchis. Meanwhile, InterCity began to build up its own strong identity in other areas, for instance, through sponsorship of sporting activities such as that of the InterCity squash championships.

Alongside these particular InterCity campaigns, BR ran its own corporate advertising, which focused on customer service initiatives and on the number of trains operated. It was perhaps a tribute to the inbuilt strength of the InterCity brand that many rail customers saw these too as being InterCity commercials. These commercials also featured the last in the long line of BR slogans; "We're getting there."

In 1986, when John Prideaux took over as Managing Director of InterCity, he and Rob Mason, who continued as

"Train Jam" TV Commercial – 1985

Marketing Director, identified the opportunity to build much more on the inherent strength of the InterCity brand. The key requirements were, firstly, to ensure that the brand was only applied in ways which were associated with high quality and, secondly, to distinguish the InterCity business much more sharply from British Rail which increasingly had negative associations for the public.

The InterCity vision

By 1990 InterCity had identified a new vision statement which was "to be the best, most civilised way to travel at speed from centre to centre." Meticulous attention to quality standards was to be paid in every way and to every aspect of InterCity trains and services. This in turn, led to

InterCity sponsored the 1985 National Squash Championships - staged on a glass-sided squash court inside Brunel's restored train shed at Bristol dating back to 1840

Examples of road-side advertising to attract the motorist

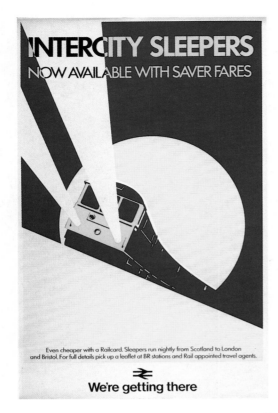

BR corporate branding at base of InterCity poster – 1986

a number of new initiatives. For instance, it was recognised that business customers in Second Class were not satisfied with the quality being offered. The very name Second Class was off-putting and a decision was taken to retitle this to "Standard".

The InterCity image

Following InterCity's lead, each of the BR businesses developed their own identity, image, and most

Pullman branding in 1990

importantly, their own marketing initiatives. In June 1986, Network SouthEast, for example, launched a massive re-branding of the London area services involving half of the BR fleet. The InterCity identity, albeit de-hyphenated, was still felt to be too closely associated with that of BR's. For example, it still used BR typeface and logo, and was ill-served in this connection in the public mind. It became obvious that there was a need to present a separate identity for InterCity. A design consultancy, Newell & Sorrell, was commissioned for this purpose and they produced the new *INTERCITY* logotype and the Swallow emblem. The emblem was specifically designed to emphasise speed and civilised movement. The new identity was launched in 1987 in time for the 21st anniversary of the InterCity brand.

'Train Magic'

By the late 1980s consumer expectations of all brands had developed significantly compared with those prevalent in the early days of InterCity. Successful brands still needed to have hard, functional benefits and InterCity clearly had these. But increasingly there was an emotional content with much more subjective associations and links. To be a successful brand in the late 1980s InterCity needed to be much stronger in this emotional area, so that customers would see the sense in choosing InterCity in an increasingly competitive market place.

InterCity identified this missing link in the idea of 'train magic'. On an InterCity train people were cocooned in an environment away from the cares of the world and could relax. This, of course, led to the famous 'Relax' advertising launched in 1988. This was totally different from anything which had gone before and made customers think of InterCity in a new way. InterCity now had a very clearly defined identity which was all its own. It was a distinctive brand building its own special relationships with its customers.

One problem with this new strategy, however, was that it could be viewed as highly elitist. There was a risk that InterCity would be seen to be a service purely for the expense account business traveller, even though two-thirds of InterCity's customers were, in reality, leisure travellers. A Marketing Manager for leisure travel was brought in to redress this imbalance. He faced a situation where InterCity was viewed by leisure travellers as expensive, poor value for money and having a complex fare structure as well.

Immediate actions were taken to review the price structure and to improve the ways in which prices were communicated. People were not interested in the structure. They were only interested in the price they had to pay. As a result, attractive, low-priced Apex fares were extended to a range of long-distance journeys around the country. For the longer term, a revenue management initiative was developed which enabled a much wider range of attractive leisure fares to be had without their being a risk of over-

'Relax' TV commercial

crowding. The new approach extended beyond pricing in that InterCity's advertising and promotion was consciously pushed towards the needs of the leisure market.

Apex poster, emphasising the price, as displayed on the London Underground

Corporate name and consumer brand

By 1990, InterCity had become clearly established as one of the top 150 businesses in the United Kingdom. Marketing success had been a key element in its move into profitability. The brand was now performing two roles; firstly, it was a corporate name and, secondly, it was a consumer brand in the market place. In addition, it became possible to develop sub-brands within the total InterCity business, such as Pullman and First Class.

Although clearly a national brand, InterCity was also important to local communities and local markets who were proud of their link with the national network. These local differences were reflected in the organisation of InterCity marketing, where there were teams for national activities as well as for each geographical route. For example, the InterCity Apex fare from Glasgow to London was initiated on the West Coast route and became a £30m national product. InterCity in Scotland was re-launched because it was felt important for InterCity to have a strong presence in the very competitive Anglo-Scottish travel market.

As so often before, the development of InterCity's image was linked inexorably to the introduction of new trains. The InterCity 225 was inaugurated on the Leeds to London route in 1989. However, it was consciously decided to hold back the the main promotion until the service was extended to Newcastle and Edinburgh in 1991. Indeed, by 1991 InterCity was sufficiently closely associated in the public mind with the 'Relax' image that it was felt that its advertising could go back to InterCity's roots and promote speed and modernity. In addition, the British people could be reminded that InterCity was something to be proud of. Research demonstrated that InterCity ran more trains at over 100mph than any other railway in Europe and this fact went on to become the basis of new advertising.

Based on this strategy, the so-called 'Black Silk' commercial was used to launch the InterCity 225, the epitome of InterCity's strength of speed, frequency, comfort and modernity. It proved to be an effective campaign and research demonstrated a significant and positive impact on customer attitudes.

InterCity "Relax" Television Commercial Awards

One of advertising's best loved campaigns which received many accolades

Creative Circle 1989

"The Big One" (Gold of Golds)
Silver Award – Best Idea in 40 seconds
Gold Award – Best Direction
Silver Award – Best Use of Animation
LWT Honour Best TV Commercial (Silver)

Designers and Art Directors Association 1989

Silver Award for the Best 40 second TV Commercial
Nomination of Most Outstanding Use of Music
Nomination of Best Direction

British Television Advertising 1989

Gold Award for Travel

Institute of Marketing 1989

TV Leisure (Gold)
Complete Campaign (Gold)

Cannes 1989

Lion D'Argent – Travel Category
Travel Advertising Award 1989

Travel Advertising Awards 1989

TV Leisure – Gold
TV Business – Silver
Complete Campaign

International Monitor Awards 1989

Best Achievement
Best Director

London International Advertising Awards 1989

Best Director
Best Transportation
Best Music and Lyrics

Golden Break Awards 1989

Gold Break Award – Gold of Golds
Golden Break – Best Use of Music
Golden Break – Best Director

Travel Advertising Awards 1990

Best Radio Commercial (Highly Commended)
Best Business Campaign, Press (Silver)

'Black Silk' giant poster hoarding supports TV and Press campaign 1991/2

Deep recession: great ideas

By now the British economy was yet again deep in recession and InterCity, like virtually every other business, was badly affected. Thus the joint Boots' promotion was launched at the same time as the InterCity 225 was fully introduced. This promotion has enabled three million people to travel at half price over two years. It also generated over £6m extra income for the InterCity business and created much goodwill in the leisure market.

Other initiatives unfortunately have had to be curtailed. For example, the 'Frequent Traveller' programme for business travellers failed to meet its initial targets and could not be maintained in the harsh economic climate. Looking back, there must be considerable regret that such a potentially powerful customer loyalty programme is not currently available to InterCity to compete with the many 'Air Miles' offers.

In January 1992, Chris Green came to InterCity as Managing Director determined that the InterCity brand and image would continue to strengthen and develop. A key area for this development was in the customer service arena. In 1988 Senior Conductors had been introduced, whilst the 1989 strategy study proved that the onboard catering service was a necessary and integral part of the InterCity product and needed significant upgrading.

Chris Green felt that InterCity was still lacking the personal touch that airlines regularly achieved. He then gave customer service a new and forceful impetus in order to create a more welcoming, caring and accessible image. This was achieved through the introduction of the customer welcome teams, the telesales operation and the launch of the 1993 InterCity Shuttle on the shorter

distance, high frequency routes. Similarly, new colours (claret and blue) were used to emphasise the new, warmer, more approachable image that InterCity wished to create.

Boots joint promotion generated £6m new business for InterCity

The Shuttle logo

'Welcome'

To support this new direction, a radically different advertising campaign was planned and top advertising agencies were asked to pitch for the business. Saatchi and Saatchi once again won the contract with the simple word 'Welcome' and the 'Welcome to a City – Welcome to InterCity' campaign. It emphasised customer service but it also built on the slightly surreal 'train magic' approach of 'Relax'. It proved to be another highly successful campaign with follow-up research showing that customers really recognised that InterCity was becoming a more friendly and welcoming way to travel.

During 1992, it became clear that the Government's railway privatisation plans would have a significant impact on InterCity both as a business and as a brand, although the Government repeatedly emphasised its commitment to the InterCity brand as a national asset. However, the announcement on 3rd February 1993 that three InterCity routes (Gatwick, East Coast and Great Western) were to be among the first routes to be privatised sounded the death knell for InterCity as a single business. This did not necessarily mean the end of the InterCity brand however, and the Government recognised that the brand was too important to the railway industry to be allowed to simply slip away. In turn, customers wanted the reassurance that the qualities that had always been embodied in InterCity would be maintained and developed. Future franchise operators would have to spend a great deal of money to build a brand of their own to match InterCity's impact in the market place. The politicians realised that it would be ironic if British Rail's greatest marketing success was lost as an early result of a policy which aimed to create more innovative marketing of the railway.

InterCity Shuttle; identification symbol at St Pancras

The brand in an uncertain future

The rail industry has entered a new period when there will be no integrated InterCity business but there will be an InterCity brand. It will continue to guarantee fast, high quality, comfortable, long-distance train services. Apart from 'Gatwick Express', the brand will cover all of the InterCity network that had previously been operated as one integrated business. British Rail has agreed to continue to use the InterCity brand as long as the routes involved are managed by the Board. Beyond that, it seems likely that franchised routes will wish to use InterCity as an endorsement of their services. A Marketing Services Company has been set up, led by John Cimelli, which will provide brand management services to all users.

In conclusion, it is clear that the InterCity brand has become a major success. Its customers in this country say so and it has been copied around the world. This success is a tribute to the hard work and creativity of many people who have worked on developing the brand over the last twenty-eight years. Although the future will be very different, let us hope that the next 28 years bring a similar record of innovation and development of brand, image and design. ✈

Figurative theme for poster and TV campaign – 1992

TV commercial mimics the GTI car ads whilst selling InterCity's competitive advantages – 1994

Giant poster series promotes train frequency

An IC225 leaves Newcastle with a Kings Cross-Glasgow train

Chapter Five

BETTER BY DESIGN

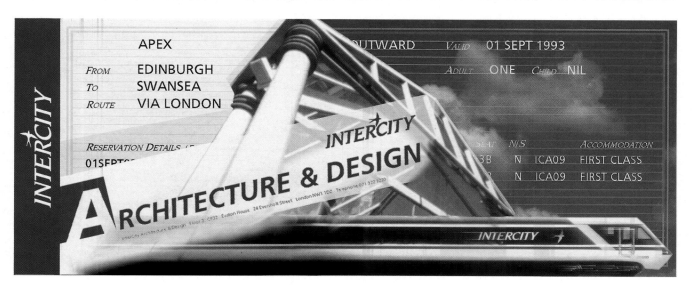

It was the much maligned Dr Beeching who wrote an article in the Financial Times in April 1964 announcing that the Design Panel was engaged upon the development of an extensive new BR corporate image. A year later in 1965 the new Corporate Identity was launched and proved to be one of the most extensive and successful post-war design initiatives. It brought a strong sense of order and uplift to trains, road vehicles, uniforms, stations, signs and marketing.

With a stimulating mixture of external and internal talent, the Design Panel operated continuously from 1965 to 1994 and had its foundations in Sir Brian Robertson's 1956 Design Panel initiative. It was responsible for spotting opportunities for innovative design in such varied projects as the exterior shape of the High Speed Train, the glorious reconstruction of Liverpool Street station and, for the InterCity story in particular, the challenge of the emerging InterCity brand application.

In simple terms, design is the way in which a company presents itself to the consumer. It represents the external face of an industry and a quality business has the opportunity to reinforce this important fact to its potential customers through quality design. As InterCity became increasingly aware that it needed to position itself at the quality end of the travel market, it was natural that it

Design is the way in which a company presents itself to the consumer

played a major role in harnessing the Design Panel's potential.

Early BR corporate identity

In 1966 the emphasis was on creating a single corporate identity for British Rail since, at that time, InterCity was no more than a brand name for the newly-electrified Euston to Liverpool and Manchester services. The corporate identity was crowned with the genius of the double arrow symbol which came to have European recognition as a symbol for railways. A specially-designed Rail Alphabet was introduced which was to stand the test of time for both clarity and style. It has been widely copied – inside and outside the transport industry.

It was undoubtedly helpful to the emerging InterCity that the clutter of regional liveries based on bygone days should be swept away and replaced by a national colour scheme. This not only brought acceptance for network branding but actually gave InterCity an early sub-brand. Whilst multiple units and locomotives were progressively painted in a new rail blue, express trains were picked out from 1966 in a more dashing and streamlined colour scheme using a striking blue and grey livery. This was a

An HST in early corporate livery with the original Inter-City brand name

milestone in InterCity's design history since it was the beginning of a nationally branded fleet of long-distance passenger services. Bringing this excellent design into service as part of the prestigious 1966 electrification brought a powerful lesson to the railways that good design was good business.

A Class 50 in large logo blue livery, April 1984

Locomotive liveries

Over the 28 years from 1966 to 1994, a number of different liveries have been applied to BR's locomotives. Prior to 1966 most diesel locomotives had emerged from the workshops in various shades of green – a throw-back to the days of steam. A few Western Region 'Warship' and 'Western' diesel-hydraulics had daringly entered traffic in maroon, while others wore truly experimental liveries such as golden ochre or desert sand. These

elegant applications of colour undoubtedly led to a greater awareness of the value of train liveries in marketing rail travel.

After mid-1966, rail blue was gradually applied to locomotives, either as they were delivered from the manufacturers or as they passed through main workshops for repainting. This changeover to rail blue was a long process with some green locomotives surviving into the early 1980s. Rail blue remained the corporate BR locomotive colour until the mid 1980s when various new schemes were accepted and separate business identities authorised.

InterCity 125 livery with the revised wrap-round red stripe on the left-hand train at Paddington in 1990

The first nameplate in InterCity claret. It has become InterCity's custom to present a third plate to the sponsor. Managing Director Chris Green, Chris Heaps and the President of The Law Society at the naming of No. 90013 at Euston in October 1992

Locomotive names

For the Queen's Silver Jubilee in 1977, a new naming policy was introduced, firstly as a corporate venture and then latterly by the business sectors. As a corporate operation a number of locomotives hauling all types of trains, both passenger and freight, were named. However, in more recent InterCity times the business named its own locomotives and therefore the choice of names and locomotive types became much more selective. Cast nameplates were originally adopted using the standard Rail Alphabet. On the formation of InterCity as a business, thin polished aluminium plates were used. These did not prove popular as they appeared less prestigious than their predecessors and from 1992 cast plates have again been employed. Since the introduction of claret as the InterCity house colour in 1992 many plates have been repainted in this shade to emphasise brand consistency.

Designing the InterCity Brand

The Inter-City name (with a hyphen) appeared on trains from 1966 until the mid 1980s. InterCity Sleepers were branded in 1969 but the major design opportunities were to arrive with the HST and the APT in the 1970s. In 1972, the prototype HST was fully branded in BR corporate style, whilst the production trains retained the blue and grey colour scheme with the InterCity brand name. However, it was sectorisation in 1982 that strongly developed the InterCity brand and this in turn brought about the appearance of some dramatic new liveries. The APT had been operating in one of the most strikingly attractive liveries ever applied in Britain and in October 1983 this became the basis of the new livery of the emerging InterCity business.

The APT was the first train to carry the new InterCity livery

This new livery was based on a light grey with a strong dark grey band through the windows held together by a bold red and white stripe that ran the whole length of the train and locomotive. There were always problems with the front end design of trains as safety agreements required a substantial yellow front to be included in addition to the provision of headlights. The problem was ultimately solved on the HST with an elegant compromise that allowed the red line to wrap right round the cab and run back along the train.

In 1987 InterCity celebrated its 21st birthday with an announcement regarding further refinements in the design of its livery. The new branding was to be developed by the design consultancy Newell & Sorrell who were commissioned to produce a new symbol for InterCity. The brand name from that point in time became *INTERCITY* in an italicised script whilst the new brand symbol became the swallow. The latter was given a three-dimensional form and the feeling of speed was emphasised by a striated design.

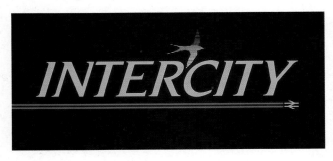

The emerging INTERCITY brand in 1987, still showing a token allegiance to BR

Rolling stock design

Continuous application of good design to the exterior of trains has brought improvement to the point where Britain can claim to have one of the best designed passenger railway fleets in Europe. The evidence can clearly be seen in the progress from the box-like electric locomotives of the 1960s to the West Coast Class 90, to the East Coast Class 91 and finally to the beautiful InterCity 250 where form sadly got ahead of funding in 1992.

The interior of trains had enjoyed similar attention to design detail and full-size mock-ups were regularly used to get every detail right. It took over a year to design the interior of the Mark IV coach, but even a brief glance at the progress from the Mark I designs of the 1950s provided the justification for all the hard work that continuous progress entailed. The Mark III coach of the 1970s offered a bright, no-fuss interior with high standards of lighting.

By the time of completion of the East Coast electrification in 1991, the new InterCity 225 was offering a much more sophisticated and reserved interior colour scheme in various shades of grey. Glass partitions and offset central corridors divided First Class coaches into smaller, more intimate bays whilst subdued lights gave a more relaxed atmosphere. Standard accommodation gave a bright and friendly interior with the emphasis on aircraft-type seating arrangements.

Class 90 locomotives stand at Euston in 1990

The elegant Class 91 locomotive design integrates with the train

InterCity of the future? A model of the InterCity 250 – note the similarity to the Eurostar powercar

Experimental refurbishment of Mark III First Class (left) and Standard (right) vehicles in 1993

Recent refurbishment work

Since the formation of InterCity, refurbishment programmes have been undertaken during engineering overhauls aimed at updating the customer environment. InterCity launched a major £57m initiative in 1993 to develop the total refurbishment of the huge InterCity Mark III fleet over a ten year period. Two market test vehicles were designed and trialled on The Master Cutler, the Cornishman and the Golden Hind. The object was to meet customer needs for the nineties and beyond, and to ensure that InterCity retained a smart, modern image in a period where a lack of funding prevented the delivery of entirely new vehicles.

The refurbishment offered internal destination indicators in all coaches linked to a satellite tracking facility which provided automatic updates on the journey. It also offered illuminated 'Reserved Seat' signs in place of paper labels. In addition, the refurbished coaches provided jackplugs for radio and CD channels, upgraded toilets and greatly improved interior furnishings. The designs had been completed in time for the new train operating and rolling stock companies to exploit opportunities for early improvements to their products.

Designing for the customer

Design was not only about the more obvious rolling stock products. It was about creating an InterCity house style which flowed smoothly from stations to stationery and from tickets to trains. As part of the Welcome initiative launched by Chris Green in 1992, design was in the lead again with the decision to upgrade the InterCity brand still further to include more warm and welcoming colours. Focused around a warm claret colour, this was added to the palette to reinforce the reigning classical but cold range of greys and blacks. Because of its associations, claret became identified as the visible symbol for InterCity customer service. The new Welcome teams wore the claret uniforms first and they created a highly-visible impact. The new porters at Kings Cross followed and then the entire On Board Service staff changed over to claret in less than a year.

The existing station signs were edged in claret to give them a warmer feel

Interior design progression 1950s-1990s

Mark I

Maximum speed 90mph as built, some were upgraded to run at 100mph. Introduced from the early 1950s, this was the first of the standard designs. This shows the First Class configuration

Mark II

Maximum speed 100mph InterCity's second generation coach. Introduced from the mid 1960s, this was the workhorse of the fleet until the advent of Mark III. View of original Second Class seating in the later air – conditioned version

Mark III

Maximum speed 125mph. Introduced from 1976 with the High Speed Train. Air-suspension, air-conditioning and bright cheerful interiors contributed to the instant success of the HST; this is refurbished Standard accomodation

Mark IV

Maximum speed 140mph. The latest in InterCity's fleet introduced for the East Coast electrification. This view of Standard seating also shows the inwards slope to the bodyside to accommodate a tilt train profile should it become desirable in the future

Elsewhere, the warmer welcoming message was fully integrated – sometimes in the physical product and sometimes in more general design. New signing included large illuminated running-in name boards to help customers on arriving trains. Clocks, seats, indicators, lamp-posts and Shuttle desks were all highlighted in the friendly InterCity claret. Euston station was totally upgraded as a major flagship terminal to act as a working model for other main stations and promptly won the 1994 UK Best Station award. The basic design principles were also applied to media presentations and sales literature to reinforce the business quality message. Examples ranged from television advertisements to the redesign of seat reservation labels to match the train interiors.

A message that time matters - encased in warm claret

Clarity and simplicity of train time and destination information is essential at busy InterCity stations and the many forms of traditional platform information signs have been replaced as far as possible with specially designed clusters of the much more versatile CCTV information screens. In turn, flap and dot-matrix main departure indicators are being replaced by banks of similar screens.

A train indicator for arrivals and departures

For many InterCity customers the opportunity to take a snack or meal on the train is very much part of the total travel experience and for some may well be the deciding factor in favour of rail against the coach or private car. Consequently both the catering product and package have been redesigned to reflect this new quality with a strong InterCity branding throughout – whether on the packaging and labelling of sandwiches or the highly-successful design of carrier bags which brought some care and order to train tidiness.

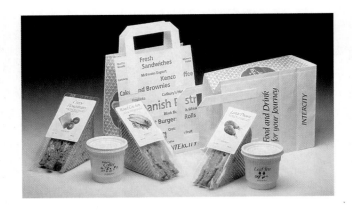

Strong branding for quality products

The InterCity map, showing at a glance all InterCity routes and the main stations served, will surely go down in history, along with the HST, as an icon of good railway design comparable to the stylised London Transport Underground map. It evolved from a complex diagrammatic map into an art form which reinforced InterCity's overall quality image.

The 1987 version of the InterCity map - the first to carry the swallow

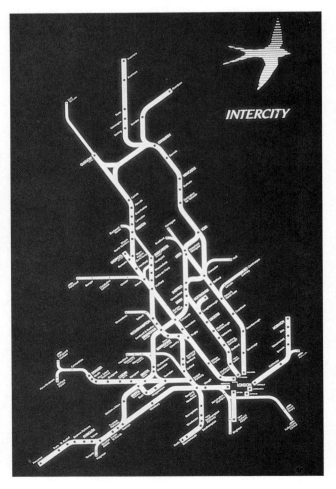

An elegant design for the InterCity Shuttle desk at Euston

More distinctive new uniforms for Senior Conductors were a landmark in 1989

Refurbished concourse at Carlisle

New Travel Centre at Reading

Good design is good business

Good design has been at the core of the InterCity brand since its earliest days in 1966. InterCity was always seen as the stylish, highly acceptable face of British Rail and good design frequently helped it to position itself with its commercial competitors in the market place as a product of quality. InterCity's name, image and design have been unashamedly copied throughout the world. The challenge will now fall upon the future new train companies to maintain and build on the design quality of the 1990s.

It was encouraging that in late 1993 one of the first acts of the new Gatwick Express train operating company was to extend the powerful, InterCity concept of branding to its logical conclusion by providing a unifying colour for its uniforms, its trains and its stations – even down to the replacement of the red line on the trainside with a matching claret stripe. This was very much in the spirit of the 1964 alliance between design and marketing – Dr Beeching would have been proud of the enormous progress made. ✈

Gatwick Express in the new 1993 livery

Caring for the traveller is at the core of InterCity's customer service

Stations to stationery

Tickets to trains

Number on Map   **Depot**

1. Long Rock (Penzance)
2. Laira (Plymouth)
3. Bath Road (Bristol)
4. St Philips Marsh (Bristol)
5. Landore (Swansea)
6. Oxley (Wolverhampton)
7. Etches Park (Derby)
8. Longsight (Manchester)
9. Neville Hill (Leeds)
10. Heaton (Newcastle)
11. Craigentinny (Edinburgh)
12. Polmadie (Glasgow)
13. Crown Point (Norwich)
14. Wembley (London)
15. Willesden (London)
16. Bounds Green (London)
17. Edge Hill (Liverpool)
18. Holyhead
19. Inverness
20. Aberdeen
21. Wolverton

○ Maintenance Depot

● Servicing Depot

☐ British Rail Maintenance Ltd (BRML)

Map of InterCity Maintenance and Servicing Depots

Chapter Six

FLEET OF FOOT –
INTERCITY'S TRAINS

To many people the IC125 is the epitome of InterCity

InterCity's character has always been closely associated with its fleet of locomotives and rolling stock and has always been at the glamorous end of the railway spectrum. The very nature of its business required it to have the most powerful and sophisticated trains. It is interesting to observe how InterCity took over the traditional locomotives of the 1960s and, from the 1970s, evolved them into its own specialist fleet with the High Speed Train, the IC225 and ultimately the beautiful IC250 design.

This demonstrated that InterCity was becoming a more cohesive organisation and was increasingly being driven by cost effective business management as well as by engineering reliability. Indeed, so successful was the policy that the wedge-shape profile of the HST cab remains one of the most widely recognised symbols of InterCity. It is important, therefore, to consider how the streamlined InterCity fleet of today emerged from the hotch-potch series of designs resulting from the 1955 Modernisation Plan.

The locomotive fleet

In 1966, the locomotives and rolling stock used on InterCity's services were a decidedly mixed bag and, although steam traction was due to be withdrawn just two years later, around 1,000 main line steam locomotives were still available for use.

Introduced for the birth of InterCity, the Class 86 electric locomotive was for many years the mainstay of the West Coast route. This example, painted in corporate Rail Blue, leaves Crewe in 1985

The diesel traction fleet consisted of around 2,600 locomotives in 1966. These were used for many types of operation ranging from InterCity trains to humble pick-up freights. Most of the diesel locomotives were built as a result of the 1955 Modernisation Plan, but some second generation diesel classes were in use by 1966 and these tended to have been designed in less haste and with more horsepower.

For the introduction of the 'New Railway' from Euston to Liverpool and Manchester, modern electric locomotives were introduced in the 1960s with no less than five mini-fleets built by different manufacturers. These were followed by a much-needed standard locomotive, then known as AL6 – now Class 86. By the end of 1966, 340 main line electric locomotives were in service but not all of these were used on InterCity duties.

By 1982, 3,800 coaches were needed to operate InterCity services. Today, almost the same number of trains are run with just 2,400 – a reduction of over one third in just over ten years. This was impressive productivity by any standard. Higher stock utilisation was achieved by standardising train formations, improving turnrounds and above all, by investing in Driving Van Trailers to allow introduction of 'push-pull' working. These visible changes were also supported by the much less visible 'sweating' of assets

at depot level to achieve improved productivity.

Control of the assets

By the 1990s, maintenance schedules were geared to keeping trains in service during the daytime by focusing all possible maintenance on the night hours. An 18-hour working day was commonplace for individual trainsets and routinely involved sets running between 800 and 1,000 miles per day. The best examples achieved up to 1,400 miles a day on the long-haul runs to and from Scotland.

Computer control systems such as Total Operations Processing System (TOPS) and Passenger Operational Information System (POIS) offered new opportunities to get a tighter grip on the passenger fleet. These systems led to the introduction of precise mileage-related maintenance schedules instead of the previous, somewhat looser time-related maintenance. A conservative estimate was that productivity had improved by at least 10% as a result of stronger asset management. Where trainsets were previously given an extensive monthly overhaul regardless of whether they had travelled ten or thirty thousand miles, the new system only invested in this expensive activity when the full mileage had been achieved.

The POIS system also improved defect management by offering rapid reporting and swift analysis of defects. The introduction of data-link radio messages was a creative development from the Anglia team. It enabled Senior Conductors to give real-time reporting of faults in traffic by using a bar code which triggered an immediate printout at the home depot. The maintenance engineers were therefore ready with the right staff and equipment to carry out repairs as soon as the trains rolled into their depots at night. On the Class 91 electric locomotive, an on-board computer logged any technical problems which arose during the day's running and depot staff could take a read-out from this log before the locomotive was serviced. The latest development, trialled on some HST power cars, was for this information to be relayed by satellite to the depot.

InterCity did not take direct control of its locomotive fleet until the mid 1980s and prior to this, locomotives were managed on a common user basis controlled by BR's Operations department. The introduction of a dedicated InterCity locomotive fleet, together with fixed-formation train working, brought a new attention to detail which in turn led to increased reliability and an improvement in the 'miles per failure' performance indicator.

InterCity coaches
There had been significant improvements in quality since the first Mark I coaches of the early 1950s. The first air-conditioned vehicles were introduced in 1971 (Mark IId) and within twenty years all regular, daytime InterCity services were composed of air-conditioned stock. The benefits of air-conditioning were noise reduction and a controlled environment for the customer with energy savings for InterCity.

Other improvements over the years have included the replacement of steam-heated by electrically-heated coaches, the replacement of vacuum braking by air brake and the introduction of disc brakes which were critical in the move towards much higher speeds. Over the last forty

State of the art InterCity 225 bogie for 140 mph running. Note the disc brakes

years bogie design has developed from the BR1 basic bogie with its plain bearings and 90 mph top speed through to the air-suspended 125 mph BT10 bogie and the 140 mph Swiss-designed bogie fitted to IC225 vehicles. Each step in the development of bogie design has led to improved riding qualities and a reduction in costs.

InterCity coaches needed a heavy overhaul about every ten years and this became the opportunity to refurbish the interiors, both in terms of decor and materials for the benefit of customers. A refurbishment of the Mark III fleet took place over the 1984-90 period and a more radical refurbishment is being developed for the late 1990s.

From the beginning of 1994, InterCity's fleet of 'slam-door' coaches was being equipped with Central Door Locking, in the form of a secondary bolt operated by air pressure. When the train is ready to leave the station the Senior Conductor activates the system. It is only released when the train reaches its next station stop – and only then on the platform side of the train. Once released doors can be opened by passengers in the normal way.

Developments in high speed trains
The fleet of 125 mph HSTs had always been central to InterCity's commercial performance. In the 1960s the pursuit of higher speeds on existing tracks gave its engineers two demanding technical challenges. Firstly, Britain had to enter the high speed railway market with diesel power because only one of the five InterCity routes was at that time electrified. Secondly and more funda-mentally, the new high speed train would have to run within the constraints of the existing infrastructure. The British railway network was the first in Europe to be completed and its main alignments were generally determined a century or more ago, well before railway engineers had begun to plan for today's very high speeds.

A tight fit on West Coast infrastructure at Linslade Tunnel near Leighton Buzzard

Whilst IC125s and later IC225s stole the limelight, Mark II locomotive-hauled coaches were the workhorses of InterCity for more than a decade

Such is the intense utilisation of the InterCity fleet that routine maintenance – ranging from technical checks to everyday cleaning – has to be carried out mostly at night

Evolution of the Driving Van Trailer; from converted Mark II coaches used on the Anglia route (left) to the custom-built version used on IC225 (right)

In June 1972 the prototype InterCity 125 was rolled out. This train epitomised what railway engineers regarded as the key to success when applying technical innovation to meet the ever-growing demands of the commercial market place. The philosophy was best summed up in the motto – 'keep it simple, build it fast'.

The world's fastest diesel

The InterCity 125 took available technology and created an entirely new package which represented a step-change in passenger rail travel. From the outset the train adopted air suspension, improved braking and electronic traction control for smoother levels of acceleration. The train was designed as a fixed formation unit with a power car at either end. The enormous success that followed the train's introduction is now history. The production InterCity 125s inaugurated the world's fastest diesel-powered rail services in 1976.

Having proved the commercial benefits of high speed with InterCity 125 and with 110 mph electric traction on the West Coast, InterCity was able to show that electrification of the London to Edinburgh route would produce the required 7% return on investment demanded by the Government at the time. In June 1984 East Coast electrification was authorised and important strategic decisions had to be taken on locomotives and rolling stock which would be in service until at least 2020.

The analysis considered ways of reducing the capital cost of traction by adopting the concept of a non-powered Driving Van Trailer (DVT) at one end of the train, whilst the locomotive stayed at the other end. The train could then be driven from either end but with only one locomotive which would be remotely controlled when pushing.

Productivity of the assets was a second key issue and after considerable debate it was decided that the traction unit should be detachable for use on other services such as parcels and overnight services. As it had become a locomotive again, the new type was given the classification Class 91.

Maintaining operating flexibility was the third major area of analysis and although the train was to run in fixed formation for push-pull passenger duties, a decision was taken not to purchase articulated coaches where adjacent coaches share a common bogie, as in the case of the APT and the TGV. This meant that defective coaches could be more easily removed, so reducing the risk of having to cancel a complete train.

Thanks to the APT project, preliminary work had already been carried out by the Mechanical & Electrical Engineering Department on a new generation high speed train for the East Coast. The new train was to be even more versatile than the InterCity 125 and included a body profile which would give it tilt capability for the future. The new train was born and finally christened 'InterCity 225' to emphasise its 225 km/h (140 mph) design speed.

In putting together the business and technical specifications for the new train, the aim was neither to procure the fastest, most technically advanced train nor was it to build the most luxuriously appointed train. The challenge was to improve on the already highly successful East Coast HSTs at an affordable price and within a relatively short timescale. The InterCity 125 was already the fastest and most successful diesel train in the world. Product development had therefore to be calculated on a step-by-step basis rather than by quantum leap. Coming in the wake of the ill-fated APT, British Rail could not afford another commercial failure with the InterCity 225.

One significant outcome of the APT experience was the extension of engineering knowledge on a number of fronts, such as vehicle dynamics which enabled performance specifications to be significantly improved. Additionally, important lessons were also learned about project management particularly in respect of tighter control and clearer accountability.

East Coast IC225

InterCity 225 was made a free-standing project with its own Project Director, David Rollin, who was directly responsible to the Managing Director. The project also had its own engineer who was responsible for all technical matters and who, in turn, reported directly to the Project Director. These fundamental decisions gave the project a sharp focus of responsibility which was a major ingredient in its final success.

British Rail's overall procurement policy was also changing as the InterCity 225 went out to tender. Traditionally BR had designed its own locomotives and rolling stock which were then manufactured in its own workshops. Specifications and procurement of bought-in material such as traction equipment was also handled by BR, as was the management of the project. Due to its

inherent weaknesses, this arrangement had become increasingly out of step with the requirements of the BR businesses whose primary concern was with the commercial performance of the InterCity 225. The time had come to break the mould. For the first time in many years it was decided that a complete project would be put out to competitive tender.

Potential suppliers bid not on the basis of BR's design as had happened previously, but on a common performance specification. The successful bidder then became the main contractor responsible for delivery to time, budget and specification under the management of the BR Project Director and his team. This radical rethink of procurement policy was taking place at the same time as wholesale change in the railway supply industry. BR was preparing to sell its manufacturing organisation British Rail Engineering Limited (BREL) to the private sector and, during the lifetime of the InterCity 225 project itself, that company went through a period of international merger.

The task of directing a £150m capital investment project could not have been accomplished without the Board empowering the project team to act independently. From the outset, the team had this authority. Thus the InterCity 225 project pioneered a new and clearly effective style of *business-led* project management. Fundamental ingredients to success were a clear project definition with measurable objectives; a dedicated yet

HSTs continued to run 'under the wires' after the East Coast electrification.

Keeping the trains running – Bounds Green Depot

Bounds Green depot started life in the late 1930s as a carriage repair shop for the LNER. It changed little until the mid-1970s when a large six-track HST depot was added to the repair shop. The most recent modernisation phase was carried out in 1988 with electrification of the yard and the six-track servicing/maintenance depot and the installation of extra jacks and overhead cranes for Class 91 maintenance.

The IC225 fleet is based at Bounds Green and many trains are serviced here overnight. Trains leave Kings Cross and pass Ferme Park (the HST fuelling point) en route to the automatic washing plant. Here the controlled emission toilets are also emptied. From the washing plant, trains take a flyover across the East Coast main line to Bowes Park where they reverse before entering the north end of Bounds Green depot.

The servicing and maintenance depot is the main production area where routine cleaning and maintenance is undertaken, with some examination and cleaning being done during the day. A variety of facilities is provided across the depot from side pits, centre pits, air supplies, hot and cold water, electricity and an ample supply of regularly used consumables for cleaners and maintenance staff. Major repairs and planned vehicle overhauls take place in the twelve-berth heavy repair shop.

Locomotives receive examination and can have component changes from pantograph to complete bogies or transformer. Coaches have repairs to modular equipment such as air conditioning and static converters and every three years are overhauled receiving replacement bogies and associated brake equipment.

Bounds Green is the home of thirty one Class 91 locomotives, 314 Mark IV coaches and around 100 vehicles of the InterCity Special Train Unit. These consist of Mark I and air-conditioned Mark II day coaches and Mark III sleepers, providing the depot with a wide variety of work. Bounds Green employs just under 300 staff and work takes place throughout the three shifts for 363 days each year.

THE SERVICING/MAINTENANCE PRODUCTION LINE

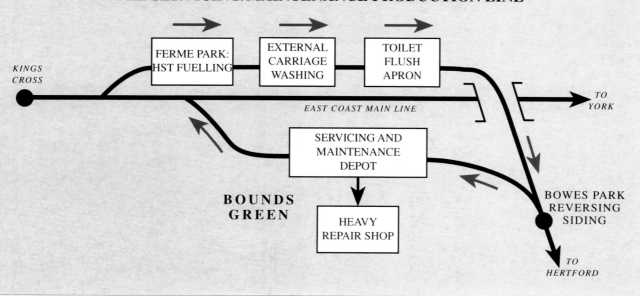

InterCity 225 – a Class 91 locomotive with Mark IV coaches

accountable project team and a number of disciplined and simple systems of control. As custodians of such large scale capital investment the project team's priority throughout was the identification and management of risk in three areas; technology, timescale and contracts.

Contracts were placed for 31 trains to cover 27 East Coast rosters and allow for maintenance. Orders were placed with GEC in January 1986 for the Class 91 locomotives at a total cost of £35m and, in December of that year, with Metro Cammell (now also part of GEC Alsthom) for the Mark IV coaches. The latter included an option to purchase additional coaches to strengthen train formations – an offer which was taken up in October 1989. After a period of shakedown trials and endurance running, the first InterCity 225 entered service on the London to Leeds route from 2nd October 1989.

Part of the track testing programme involved a 10% overspeed test. Early one Sunday morning, and in torrential rain, an InterCity 225 train reached a top speed of 162 mph and, perhaps more significantly, achieved 145 mph travelling *up* Stoke Bank between Peterborough and Grantham whereas 'Mallard' had set the world's record for steam traction going down this particular bank! When electrification was completed throughout in 1991, a record non-stop run from London to Edinburgh took place on 26th September with a total journey time of 3 hrs 29 mins. This demonstrated the potential of the route, a theme taken up later in this book.

InterCity 225 took two years to rid itself of teething problems but after that it settled down to become a popular and reliable train on the East Coast. The 225 project team were then gradually freed to develop the next challenge: the new 160 mph InterCity train.

The record-breaking 'Mallard' – 126 mph achieved in 1938

In mainland Europe very high speeds are achieved by a combination of new train technology and specially-built railways –
(above) France's 186 mph TGV and (below) Germany's 155 mph ICE

The InterCity 250

In December 1989 InterCity completed a comprehensive Strategy Review of the West Coast. This set out five basic options for the 1990s. Using the best London to Manchester time as a benchmark for the service group as a whole, the options that emerged were as follows;

1. Do nothing and keep a 2 hrs 30 mins London-Manchester journey time.

2. Accelerate and improve the reliability of the existing 110 mph trains, reducing the journey time to 2 hrs 10 mins.

3. Add some new trains capable of 140 mph with some relaxation of constraints on curves to achieve a two hour journey time.

4. Renew or upgrade infrastructure for 140-160 mph trains with minor re-alignment to remove some speed restrictions to give an overall time of 1 hr 50 mins.

5. Build a new high speed line from the Crewe area to within about 30 miles of London to cut the time to 1 hr 35 mins.

In the absence of serious capacity restraints, InterCity concluded that in the prevailing political climate, no financial case could be made for investing in a new line. Moreover, it could take up to 15 years to plan and build. At the other end of the scale the 'do nothing' option did not really exist because much West Coast signalling and track would have to be renewed in the 1990s anyway. The debate therefore focused on the middle three options which gave a range in journey times from 2 hrs 10 mins to 1 hr 50 mins.

This aerial view of Berkhamsted shows the tortuous course of the West Coast route

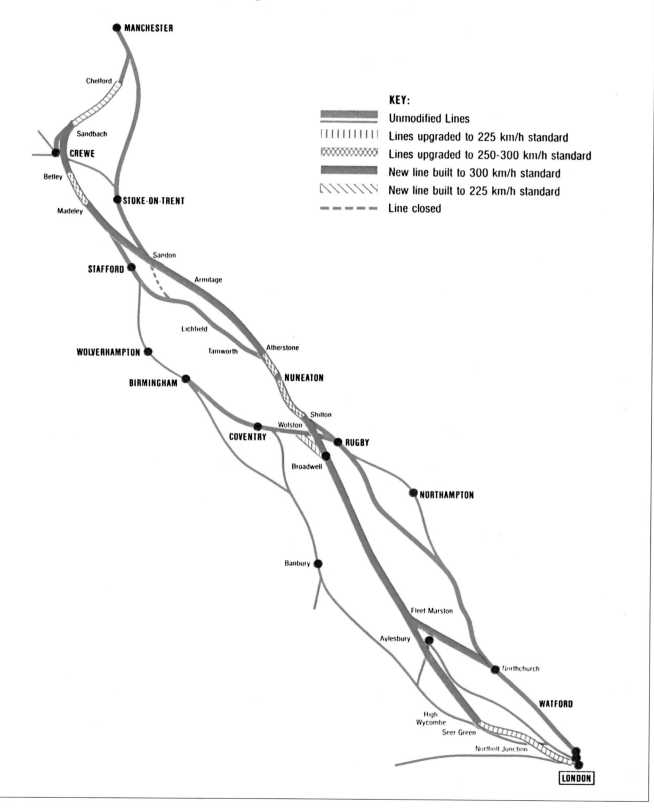

1989 Proposal for West Coast Modernisation: No. 1

Proposal for a completely new high speed route paralleling the existing route. This scheme proved not to be cost-effective and was not implemented

KEY:

Unmodified Lines
Lines upgraded to 225 km/h standard
Lines upgraded to 250-300 km/h standard
New line built to 300 km/h standard
New line built to 225 km/h standard
Line closed

MANCHESTER
Chelford
Sandbach
CREWE
Betley
STOKE-ON-TRENT
Madeley
Sandon
STAFFORD
Armitage
Lichfield
WOLVERHAMPTON
Tamworth
Atherstone
NUNEATON
BIRMINGHAM
Shilton
Wolston
COVENTRY
RUGBY
Broadwell
NORTHAMPTON
Banbury
Fleet Marston
Aylesbury
Northchurch
WATFORD
High Wycombe
Seer Green
Northolt Junction
LONDON

1989 Proposal for West Coast Modernisation: No. 2

Proposal for reconstruction of existing route with some realignment to remove long-standing speed restrictions; again this was not progressed

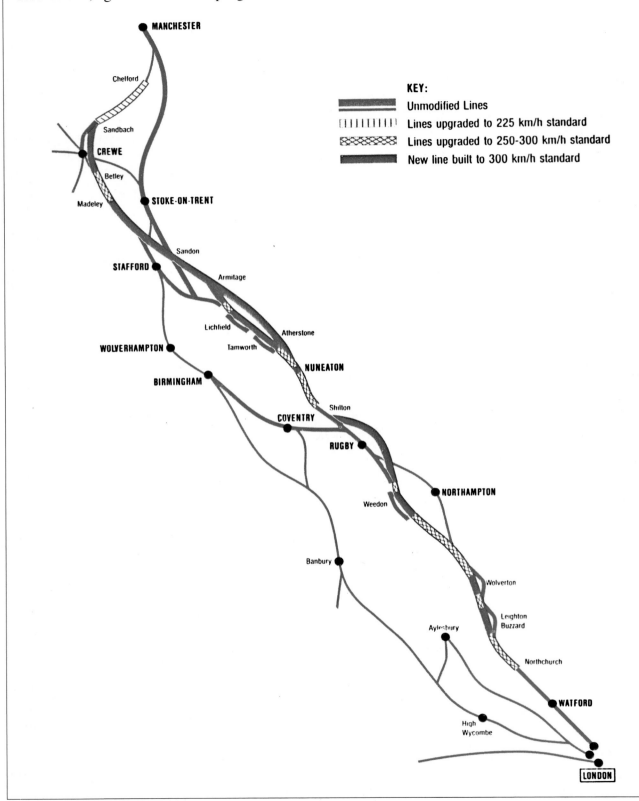

KEY:
- Unmodified Lines
- Lines upgraded to 225 km/h standard
- Lines upgraded to 250-300 km/h standard
- New line built to 300 km/h standard

The West Coast bid for IC225 trains had links with Manchester's Olympic aspirations

The key rolling stock decision was that the West Coast must get a new fleet of high performance trains if its market share was to improve. A major leap forward in speed and quality had to be achieved which would tip the competitive balance in favour of rail. The business impact of new trains had already been demonstrated in 1966 by the introduction of first-generation electric services to Liverpool and Manchester, and subsequently by the InterCity 125 and the InterCity 225. The rate of business growth, measured by both passenger volume and income, rose markedly following these events. The development of InterCity 225 demonstrated that better quality and reduced unit costs were also possible through improved train design.

A train capable of higher speeds was clearly essential for achievement of the journey times being considered on the West Coast. However, conclusions of some strategic importance were emerging from the examination of rolling stock issues. Firstly, the technical risks associated with specifying a train for speeds in the 140-160 mph range were low. The technical changes required for a high speed electric train had been incorporated in the InterCity 225 for the East Coast which had already achieved 162 mph in trials. A train with a single source of power was still seen as the best way forward.

Secondly, the business risk would actually lie in specifying too low a speed capability for the train since this would then condemn the West Coast to operate below its potential for the next 25 years. In all, the balance of financial risk favoured the specification of a train capable

of 160 mph. Thus the InterCity 250 concept was born. It was a truly evolutionary train with technical specifications derived from feedback on the best technical features, operating lessons and customer experience not only from InterCity 125 and 225, but also from European sources such as the German ICE train.

In December 1990 approval was given for the tender process to proceed and invitations to bid were released in March 1991. Following a rigorous tender evaluation exercise, a request for permission to purchase 30 InterCity 250 trains was put to the Board in December 1991.

Sadly, with the UK recession biting hard into InterCity's profits and with uncertainties arising in the shape of privatisation, funding was not forthcoming and the IC250 project was abandoned soon afterwards. West Coast has been left to operate a fleet of locomotives and coaches built predominantly in the early 1970s to cater for the far more demanding consumer standards of the 1990s.

Leasing concession

In his 1992 Autumn Statement, the Chancellor announced a Treasury concession allowing British Rail to lease rolling stock to the value of £150m over the next three years with only repayments counting against BR's External Financing Limit. Under this concession BR invited competing tenders for new trains, the competition being between InterCity 225 and Class 465/3 dual voltage Networker commuter trains for NSE's Great Northern and Kent Coast routes. Both tenders were for follow-on builds from GEC Alsthom and ABB Transportation respectively. Ironically by this time InterCity's Director, Fleet, was Brian Clementson who had developed the Networker.

The InterCity case was based on the upgrading of ten Pullman and other high earning services to InterCity 225 with a consequent cascade of Mark III coaches to displace the older fleet operating London to Birmingham services. The essence of the Government's requirements was to transfer risk to the private sector which would, if necessary, absorb the consequences of under-performance. Various options – such as outright purchase and various leasing schemes – were considered. Despite reassurances from GEC Alsthom that they had been applying a very sharp pencil to their bid, the resultant offers failed to produce any return on the investment for InterCity. Consequently, the business was unable to put forward a commercially viable leasing deal and the InterCity option was withdrawn from the competition – the West Coast modernisation had suffered yet another body blow.

It has been a long journey from the Mark I coaches of the 1950s to the InterCity 250 of the 1990s. InterCity owed its engineers much on this journey and they will be remembered not only for their technical skills but for their support in cutting costs and for carrying out so much of their work during the unsocial hours of long nights in depots. ✈

Preparing the Great British Breakfast

Chapter Seven
CATERING FOR THE CUSTOMER

InterCity's Great British Breakfast is legendary amongst early morning travellers

In 1879 the first restaurant car ran on British tracks. For 115 years the quality of railway food has been an area of lively public interest. Today the food and drink served on InterCity are arguably the best and most cost-effective anywhere in Europe. While many railways are changing over to airline-style tray meals with dishes being reheated on board, InterCity has retained a classic service in dining cars with meals freshly cooked in the train's kitchen.

Over the past few years, InterCity's catering division, On Board Services, has grown in stature. They are no longer plagued by mindless music hall jokes. Indeed, two years ago they were sufficiently confident of their expertise and experience to accept an invitation to serve British food on a top business train between Paris and Brussels and then to have the results shown on BBC television. More recently, further success came their way through tendering in partnership with the French Wagons-Lits Company and Sabena, the Belgian airline. They succeeded in obtaining the on-board contract for the Eurostar cross-Channel service between London, Paris and Brussels.

On Board Services had become a diverse £40m a year business by 1994 and was run by Terry Coyle who was previously with British Airways. Its portfolio included Pullman and Silver Standard on key business services, full-meal service on many other trains, takeaway buffets/trolleys on all others, lounge car and room service on the overnight Sleepers and catering on Special Trains.

The OBS crew-swop team boarding the early morning
Paris–Brussels train in 1992

On the latter, classic at-seat dining is an essential part of the offer for VIP private charters and for Day and Weekend Land Cruises. In addition, OBS won contracts to supply buffet or trolley services on some Network SouthEast routes and catering on the prestigious Venice-Simplon-Orient Express.

The evolution of on-train catering

The on-board catering service had long been seen as playing a very important part in the customer's perception of the total travel experience. However, viewed as a free-standing activity, on-board catering did not cover its costs and this served to fuel a debate over the acceptable subsidy for the catering service. No-one would argue that toilets on trains lose money. They were, like comfortable seats, air-conditioning, sound-proofing and good riding, part of the sum which achieved the required level of on-board ambience. But whereas there was no extra charge to use a train toilet, food and drink had always been an optional extra. The cost of an airline meal was hidden in the price of the ticket, but the cost of a rail meal was exposed for all to see.

Some catering history

With the exception of the Southern Railway who used Frederick Hotels or the Pullman Car Company, railway catering – stations and trains – was traditionally provided by the railway-owned hotels. When the railways were nationalised, the hotels were taken over by British Transport Hotels (BTH) and they also had responsibility for station and train catering. As a separate corporate entity, BTH was required to produce its own accounts. These generally showed a profit thanks to the station

buffets-which offset the trading loss on train catering.

The transformation of train catering from its post-war, low status, 'Cinderella' image to a high-quality, well-managed, professional business had its origins in two important organisational changes; the creation of the InterCity business sector and the Government directive to sell the railway hotels to the private sector.

Disposal of the hotel side of the BTH business in 1982/83 eliminated the conflicting priorities inherent in the old organisation. The station and train business, by this time trading under the 'Travellers Fare' branding, remained with British Rail. However, because of its poor image, there was considerable political pressure to sell off station and train catering. Attracted by the station trading potential, denied incidentally to BR by investment restrictions, several catering companies became interested in Travellers Fare but were deterred by its operational complexities and their own lack of experience in the on-train field.

It was now apparent that the two operations of Travellers Fare – stations and trains – were constrained in their turn by conflicting priorities. One was a potentially profitable, fast food, light meal chain, while the other was a highly specialised restaurateur with a completely different market culture inextricably tied to InterCity. In 1986 Travellers Fare's station outlets were privatised through management buyout, leaving the train business to move to its logical place within InterCity. The new unit – InterCity On Board Services (ICOBS) – was headed up by its own director who reported directly to the Managing Director, InterCity. The name was streamlined to On Board Services (OBS) in 1991.

Improving the standards

Keeping catering in-house was a good decision for it enabled InterCity to maximise its potential as an essential

Debbie Bunker, an InterCity Stewardess from Leeds, serving the Great British Breakfast to passengers on the Paris – Brussels Express in April 1992

part of its total on-board service concept. As such, it was vitally necessary to meet rising customer expectations. In the 1980s intensified competition on short – and long-haul air routes led to many improvements, the most important of which was the creation of Club or Business class travel. These new categories brought into place new standards of customer care. In turn, these became the standards by which business travellers would judge InterCity. At the same time, standards for leisure or budget-priced travellers were also being enhanced.

As a result, during the mid to late 1980s InterCity embarked on defining clear service standards for its evolving travel brands – Pullman, First Class and Silver Standard as well as for the large number of customers using the buffet and trolley services. In terms of improving standards on-board, the merits of using in-house catering as opposed to using outside catering companies had been an on-going debate. Train catering in most European countries – notably France, Switzerland, Belgium, Spain, the Netherlands and Italy – was provided by separate catering companies with the railway subsidising the operation. Only in Germany, where Deutsche Service Gesellschaft (DSG) had a role similar to

that of the former BTH, was catering provided under railway ownership. Based on the quality of service of InterCity trains in Britain and Germany, evidence suggested that an in-house operation did actually provide a better and more consistent standard of service for the customer.

Modern food service technology

While old catering cars were being replaced by new 125 mph air-conditioned coaches, organisation of the work on-board had hardly changed. Like other large caterers, BTH were able to bring new products such as frozen vegetables into their repertoire as they became available from the 1950s onwards. Apart from the cost of the vehicle itself, a charge normally borne by the train operator, the biggest cost factor in train catering was that of labour. Crew often had to be retained on a train throughout a long journey and outside normal customer mealtimes to provide a support service for the main train business.

At the start of each day, the crew would draw supplies from the store, convey them to the train in a trolley where they would be checked before loading. This routine was reasonably easy to carry out when train sets made two journeys a day with the same staff remaining on-board. But, as rolling stock productivity was raised with intensified rosters of three or four journeys a day, it was

A contrast in Buffet styles: 1960s…

…and 1990s style

not always possible to keep staff on the same train for the whole shift. This entailed changing catering crews during the course of the day when time had to be taken to stock-take so that the new crew could be satisfied that all was in order. As new train services were developed, rolling stock rosters became even more complicated, creating far more problems for the catering staff. It became normal practice for some crews to change trains once or even twice during a day's tour of duty.

Loading supplies was only the start of the day's work. Before customers could be seated, tables had to be laid, food cooked, buffet displays set-up and sandwiches made. At the end of the day everything on the car had to be cleared for destocking and unused supplies offloaded for transfer back to the depot store.

The modular approach

When it was formed in 1982, one of the early issues that had to be tackled by the new InterCity organisation was the future role of on-board catering. Given a clear business focus, the new regime began to build on the value of catering as a marketing tool. Plans included the relaunch of Pullman as the InterCity flagship for the business market; the introduction of Pullman Lounges at key stations and increased use of trolleys to provide at-seat service both in First Class and Standard accom-modation. Given a clear view of its future role, Travellers Fare worked in close association with InterCity in the short period before OBS was formed and recognised that the time was right for a major re-appraisal of new technology. External consultants were engaged and their report paved the way for the changeover to what is now known as modular catering.

By using prepared loading systems similar to those operated by the airlines, it would be possible, firstly to open buffets more quickly and for longer periods of time during each train journey and secondly, to have at-seat trolleys stocked and ready-to-go to serve all passengers at the beginning of the journey. Thirdly, restaurant services could feature a wider range of portion-controlled dishes than the current system allowed.

A further key benefit related to the refrigeration chain of supply from the depot to the vehicle which was necessary to maintain the quality of the product. The new modules were refrigerated by direct power in the depots, with the temperature maintained initially by eutectic (chilled) plates and latterly by refrigerated modules between shorebase and train.

Cook-chill

Whilst French Railways had opted for all aspects of airline-style catering including cook-chill hot dishes, InterCity wanted to maintain service flexibility, particularly with regard to a silver service breakfast. For many, it was still the factor that determined the choice of rail or an alternative mode of transport. Defying both economic and health trends, InterCity breakfast sales continued to grow to a level of around 600,000 per year, over half of all meals served. Given its importance, InterCity was not prepared to risk changes to its breakfast specification. While it was perfectly possible to produce good quality cook-chill lunch and dinner items such as coq au vin or braised beef, it was conversely very difficult to re-heat a fried egg or toast.

Accordingly, InterCity decided to go for the basic

Pullman lounges offer exclusive facilities to First Class passengers awaiting their trains

modular system with a range of cook-chill courses, but retaining the ability to cook certain critical items such as eggs, bacon, sausages, steaks and chops in the train kitchen. Equipment for this purpose, together with an automatic toasting machine capable of producing 600 items an hour, was included in the kitchen design. The traditional table layout was replaced by a tray, but the food was still silver-served onto china plates.

In the light of a trial on the West Coast between 1985 and 1987, two important adjustments were made. Firstly shorebase operations, previously in the hands of a third-party contractor, were returned to the more efficient control of OBS. Secondly, prepared meals were replaced by fresh portion-controlled food made possible by recent advances in the industry.

Modular catering was not just about changing food preparation methods, it was far more than that. It offered trolleys designed for specific tasks – chef's fridge, bar fridge, food module and trolleys for use throughout the train – all of which could be loaded onto a train in a matter of minutes.

Throughout the 24 hour period, Euston and the other West Coast shorebases were preparing the modules for the train staff when they reported for duty. Staff on board were now freed from traditional, time-consuming tasks such as washing up. After all, a large industrial machine could do a much better job in the shorebase.

Computerisation of sales and store accounting, an integral part of the modular concept, had also reduced unproductive time as well as improved stock control. Freed from these tasks, on-board staff had more time for sales and service. For far too long a successful introduction of train trolleys – a normal feature of continental trains and aircraft – had eluded Britain. They had now become an essential part of the InterCity product and this had achieved two long desired objectives; sales had increased and customers were getting catering services at their seats.

A £40 million a year business

Train catering was an inherently uneconomic activity. Because the role of train catering was to provide food for passengers on the train, its market was very much determined by the times of the trains and the travel patterns of passengers and not by the normal criteria influencing the opening hours of 'terra firma' restaurants.

For example, the 0710 Yorkshire Pullman from Leeds to Kings Cross was a well-loaded business train which served over 400 hot drinks, 100 bacon and tomato rolls and 60 to 80 cooked breakfasts during the two-hour journey. But, in order to earn its keep, the train set returned to Leeds at 1110 to start a second return journey to London at 1505. This was followed by the prestigious 1735 Yorkshire Pullman back to Leeds.

Sandwiches and light snacks were the order of the day on the two midday services, although a full service was on offer. Dinner sales on the 1735 from Kings Cross varied but around 15 to 20 was a reasonable norm. Whatever service was offered, there were always significant periods when average income dropped. Taking trolleys through

Staff training is crucial to the success of On Board Services

On Board Services uniforms – (left) In-house design work, (right) latest style in claret, 1994

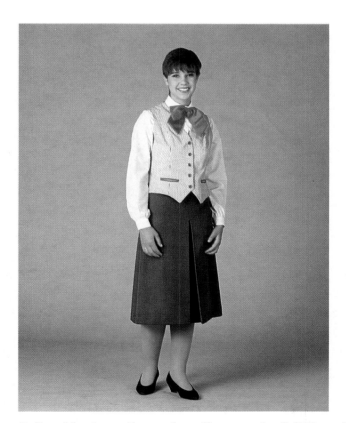 

On Board Services uniforms – for staff contracted to (left) Network SouthEast and (right) Venice-Simplon-Orient Express, 1994

InterCity chefs enter the Chef of the Year Competition supported by Terry Coyle, Director OBS

the train did increase sales significantly and helped to reduce unit costs on each train. Indeed, the snack food and drink service was profitable overall and accounted for 75% of total income.

Training and Selection

With the development of detailed service specifications on all InterCity trains, the OBS contribution to new customer care initiatives had gained momentum. A new organisation was created to deal with these new challenges. Staff recruitment and training methods were revised. New training methods were introduced including a training school based on a mock-up of a catering car.

One of the difficulties of providing staff was to find individuals who could not only manage the food, but who could also truly manage the provision of on-board service. A new on-board management role, that of Purser, has been created to complement the tasks of the Senior Conductor.

Almost in profit

In a period of seven years, train-catering turnover had risen to £40m per year whilst the internal subsidy had been reduced to 0.06% of InterCity income. The high £12.3m subsidy for 1988/89 included the cost of changing from classic to modular catering and other costs associated with shorebase management. OBS very nearly did the impossible by breaking even in 1991/92.

In the following year, 1989/90, the benefits of modular catering had started to bear fruit. Trolleys had begun to increase on-board market penetration and there was a general upturn in InterCity business. The subsidy had been reduced to 9%, the lowest in Europe. The support moved up to 14%, following a decision to give complimentary tea and coffee to Pullman passengers and complimentary light breakfast trays to customers travelling First Class in Sleepers. Complimentary tea and coffee service required

INTERCITY: NET COST OF CATERING

Year	Turnover £m	Internal Subsidy £m	Percentage of turnover
1986-87	30.6	8.1	26
1987-88	36.5	8.6	24
1988-89	38.6	12.3	32
1989-90	39.7	5.0	13
1990-91	42.9	4.8	11
1991-92	41.3	3.8	9
1992-93	40.2	5.8	14

an extra steward and, in a train environment, the life of a china cup is about 10 trips.

To put OBS figures into context the subsidy for catering on French Railways was around £29m in contrast to about £6m for InterCity.

Menu Innovation

Significant advances were also made in the range of food products offered for sale. The OBS marketing team was strengthened by the addition of an executive chef recruited from outside the railway industry. New ideas began to be developed. Revamped restaurant menus were introduced with an international emphasis replacing the traditional joints of meat for so long a feature of train meals. Roasting joints for an unknown number of customers often led to unacceptable levels of waste and dishes based on pre-portioned, extended life, products were developed.

Also, new products on the market made it possible to upgrade the quality of soups and introduce sauces (hollandaise, onion, wine, etc) hitherto difficult to make within the confines of a small kitchen. Reflecting trends in public taste, menus were now becoming much more cosmopolitan. Summer and winter menus rotated on a four-weekly cycle, and all chefs attended a training course at Westminster Catering College, prior to the introduction of new menus.

Using its purchasing clout, OBS was constantly looking out for new ideas and food items to meet changing public tastes. Planning menus for production in a small train kitchen was an on-going challenge. Each menu had a red and white meat dish, a fish dish and a vegetarian option, but the complete menu had to make use of every piece of equipment in the kitchen. For instance,

Menus feature dishes from around the world including, Chinese, Indian, Italian, Scandinavian and, of course, British

99

Sir Clement Freud and InterCity Managing Director Chris Green sample a new range of fillings at the 1992 opening of the sandwich production unit at Wigan

there had to be a grilled item, a stove top and an oven item. If all menu items were grilled dishes, the kitchen would not be able to cope. Also, the menu had to be capable of being cooked by two different methods to safeguard against failure.

Over the years, the Great British Breakfast had become a major feature of early-morning, business travel. Despite rises in prices and against all contemporary health trends, sales of this meal have continued to grow. While there was not a lot that could be done to change breakfast, OBS had managed to bring in a number of innovations. Smoked Scotch salmon with scrambled egg was, for example, offered as a main course on Pullman services as an alternative to the traditional grill tray and kippers.

Major improvements to the Buffet range

In terms of revenue generation and the number of customers that could be reached, the train buffet and trolley service generated two-thirds of receipts and, naturally enough, was very important to InterCity. Trolleys now accessed the entire train reaching many customers who preferred at-seat service and doubling demand on many routes. A significant market had been opened up, generating revenue and helping to reduce unit costs. Many new products had been added, the most important of which was the sandwich range. In the pre-

modular period, all sandwiches were made on-board in the buffet from materials supplied from the depot. Given the time taken to load and stock a restaurant car, there was often a long delay before sandwiches could be made and put on sale. Quality, moreover, was often inconsistent.

Large retailers, including Boots and Marks & Spencer, had begun selling a range of pre-packed sandwiches bought-in from specialist suppliers. Sealed in special packaging, they retained quality and product integrity for up to 36 hours. They were ideally suited for InterCity. Following a successful test on the West Coast, OBS changed over to bought-in sandwiches in 1986. The higher buying-in cost has been more than offset by the dramatic rise in sales from two to six million sandwiches a year. A national promotion of 'Celebrity Sandwiches', with fillings designed by well-known figures such as Sir Clement Freud, helped to boost sales and finally lay to rest the old jokes about stale sandwiches.

Another success had been the development of hot takeaway meals served over the buffet counter. Advances in food technology led to the development of complete meals, stored and served under refrigerated conditions which could be quickly re-heated in a microwave oven. All large stores had extensive ranges of these products. Here too was an opportunity for InterCity. Complete meals – such as chicken curry, braised beef and dumplings and vegetarian lasagne – would be offered for sale and at prices affordable by the large number of budget-conscious customers whom InterCity regarded as an important part of its market.

On Board Services use food and drink experts to advise on new products

David Small of OBS and Glyn Christian sample the re-introduced Afternoon Tea

Oz Clarke selecting some of InterCity's range of wines

On Board Services also study other caterers' methods and standards of customer service – here On Board Services and TGI Friday teams try out non-alcoholic cocktails

The Buffet provides a wide range of over 200 hot and cold snacks and drinks – OBS is the third largest sandwich retailer in the UK

All products were now branded under a family InterCity identity covering a wide range of new products such as Danish pastries, American cakes, Flapjacks, low-calorie snacks and other healthy options to satisfy the latest eating trends.

Universal, all-purpose vehicles

Over the years, InterCity had come to prefer an all-purpose catering car consisting of a small seating area and a centrally-positioned kitchen leading to a small, takeaway bar at the opposite end of the coach. This enabled staff and equipment to serve both the restaurant and the buffet. In a normal train formation, the seating part of the catering car would be next to an adjoining First Class coach which could also be used for meal service on busier trains. This was the standard configuration for all InterCity meal services.

When the IC125 was first introduced, in 1976, it was originally intended to have two separate catering cars in each eight-coach train set: a full kitchen car with twenty four First Class seats (TRUK in railway parlance) and a buffet car (TRSB) with thirty six Standard seats marshalled in the Standard end of the train. In the light of experience, it became apparent that two separate catering cars in an eight car train were more than were needed on most services. A more flexible car was introduced based on a seventeen seat saloon together with kitchen and buffet. Most of the TRUKs were converted to modular cars for the West Coast. However, because of the need to serve a large number of breakfasts in a short time span,

some Pullman services still had two separate catering cars until 1992.

Two other types of InterCity catering car should be mentioned. To provide a full, at-seat service on the very successful charters sold by Special Trains, some old Mark I catering cars, with high-capacity kitchens capable of producing 150 main meals for one sitting, have been extensively refurbished and retained in service. Apart from the Manchester Pullman stock built in 1966 for the 'New Railway', no Mark II catering cars were built. To meet the need for a small catering car for Midland Cross Country and overnight services, some Mark II coaches had a small buffet area incorporated – those used on overnight services have lounge-style seating.

Prior to the end of the present InterCity regime on 31st March 1994, the OBS organisation was route-based with the largest, located on the West Coast with a staff of around 450. The West Coast shorebase was at Euston with smaller bases at Wolverhampton, Manchester, Liverpool, Preston and Glasgow. Smaller supply points were also provided at Holyhead and Inverness. Staff covered specific trains and were kept to their regular services wherever possible in order to know their customers better. The composition of each catering crew even varied according to the level of business and covered a series of trains on a work programme known as a 'circuit'. Minimum staffing for a restaurant and buffet service was three with up to ten for a busy Pullman. To minimise stocking and destocking work, every effort was made to keep staff on the same train set throughout their working day, but there were inevitably some long days.

A catering case study on the West Coast

On the West Coast which, in OBS terms is fully modular,

The Great British Breakfast being prepared

Charter Train service sets the seal of elegance

The Purser is the on-train catering manager

crews received their modules from the shorebase trucks and checked them on to their trains. Tables were laid, kitchen activity started, the buffet set up and trolleys made ready for operation. The first two hours on a busy morning Pullman service were a period of intense activity. Typically, 60 full breakfasts may be served. This entailed cooking 120 rashers of bacon; 60 sausages and a similar number of pieces of black pudding; 90 eggs; 11 pounds of mushrooms; 12 pounds of potatoes and 10 pounds of tomatoes. Kippers were grilled to order and eggs scrambled to accompany the smoked salmon on offer. Eight loaves of bread would be toasted and two used for fried bread. Fifty pints of milk would be consumed and, with free tea and coffee now offered to all Pullman passengers, thirty gallons of hot drink would be brewed.

Except for kippers, smoked salmon and scrambled eggs which were presented on the plate, the famed Great British Breakfast Grill Tray was silver-served. All the main items, bacon, egg, sausage, tomato and fried bread, were placed on a silver platter, offered to the customer and served by spoon and fork, in classic banqueting style which is also known as 'service anglaise'. Black pudding, mushrooms and sauté potatoes were offered separately. Silver service added a touch of real elegance to an InterCity breakfast and enabled each person to have a 'customised' breakfast plate. It was in any case quite impossible to plate up 60 grill tray breakfasts in the small confines of a train kitchen.

The new OBS Company
Train catering on InterCity was organised as a centralised

activity until 1993. On-board staff and regional shorebases were route-managed, but the benefits of bulk buying, product development, funding research and facilities such as the Euston training centre were only viable on a shared basis.

From April 1994, when the various InterCity routes became train operating companies, the OBS role underwent significant change. Most of its centralised activities had been retained and passed to a new company called On-Board Supply and Service. Under this new organisation, all aspects of on-board supply would be managed up to the train side, where the work would be handed over to on-board staff employed by the train operators, much in the same way that airlines operate. OBS is also ready for early privatisation and would be purchased either through a management buyout or by an outside company. OBS in future will provide three types of commercial service; supply chain management, specialist services and on-board contract services.

Supply chain management
On the supply side, OBS will manage twenty eight shorebases in the UK with a staff of about 350. Business turnover is expected to be around £25 million a year. Its supply chain management will offer around seven hundred product lines which they will buy-in from two hundred separate suppliers. Sales will support around 1.2 million restaurant car meals; eight million sandwiches (OBS is the

A Mark I vehicle refurbished for use by Special Trains

third largest retailer in the UK); ten million soft drinks together with ten million alcoholic and twenty two million hot drinks. Essentially, they will operate very much as before. Shorebases will provide modular supplies for collection by the train companies' on-board staff; in all, those staff will deal with around two to three hundred million individual items in any one year.

Specialist Services
OBS will provide expertise in specialist areas such as food preparation and cooking, safety and hygiene, information systems and customer service training. The Euston training centre will form part of this service.

On-Board Contract Services
In the future, the twenty six train companies will be free to choose whether they prefer to operate their own on-board services or whether they wish to contract out the work to specialist firms such as OBS. On Board Services already operate on some Network SouthEast services, on Special Trains and on the Venice Simplon-Orient-Express. It will also take over the shareholding in the new Cross Channel Catering Company which was formed by InterCity in association with Wagon-Lits and Sabena to provide on-board service on the Eurostar trains between London, Paris and Brussels. This seven year contract provides a firm foundation to ensure the new OBS company has an exciting and secure future. ✈

An imaginative poster produced by the then Travellers Fare to promote All-Day Breakfast on InterCity 125 services

In 1993 Chief Steward Tony Pullin poses with his team wearing the new InterCity uniform

Chapter Eight

DELIGHTING THE CUSTOMER

A customer welcome

There can be no doubt that one of InterCity's real success stories in recent years had been the massive improvement in the quality of service on trains and at stations. The combination of a unified InterCity organised around a powerful marketing brand provided the catalyst for a series of customer service initiatives in the late 1980s and early 1990s. Having broken through the profit barrier in 1988, InterCity had to develop a business strategy to maintain that sound financial position at a time of deepening recession, falling demand and plummeting investment. The strategy agreed was one of providing enhanced customer service. In short the vision for the 1990s was one of 'delighting the customer'. A number of examples of best practice have been chosen to illustrate the great strides that the business has made in achieving that vision.

By 1990 InterCity was already well into a process of radical change that was to make it market rather than production-led. Running a railway was not just about selling tickets and running trains. Leisure customers, the most significant in volume terms, were judging InterCity by the improved standards of customer service offered not only by the airlines and coach companies but also by retail stores such as Boots, Marks & Spencer, Sainsbury and Tesco.

A total travel experience

To develop its full potential as the most civilised means of long distance travel, InterCity had to re-orientate its thinking so that its activities reflected a market-led organisation. InterCity no longer sold train trips but aimed to provide a total travel experience. This meant thinking about customers' needs, not just when they arrived at

The On Board Services stand at the Quality fair at Birmingham 1992

stations to buy tickets, but when they were sitting at home planning to make a rail journey. How did those customers want to make initial contact with the business? Was the telephone information provided adequate and welcoming? Was the route to the station well-signposted? Were secure and well-lit car parking spaces available? Was help needed on the actual station before the journey itself? Almost half of InterCity's customers travelled only once a year. Customer research showed that coping with the complexities of a busy station and searching for the right train was a daunting prospect for many would-be travellers.

Leading from the top

It was increasingly clear that a total rethink of InterCity's customer service policy for the 1990s was required. Strong leadership needed to come from the top and the newly-formed Directors' Group committed itself to a series of strategic conferences to think through the issue of maintaining market share with minimal new investment. The solution that emerged was probably one of the toughest for InterCity to manage. It recognised that there would be no hard investment-led solutions for at least five years and that the only hope for improved market share lay in switching its efforts into the softer areas of customer service. InterCity would have to go through the sort of radical culture change that British Airways had experienced in order to convert itself from a product-led

organisation into a customer-driven one. This involved convincing 30,000 InterCity staff of the need for change and then training them to meet that challenge, all within the space of just two years.

In 1988 a key initiative developed which helped to provide a firm basis for the development of customer service excellence within BR. The 'Quality Through People' initiative (QTP), was launched by the British Railways Board, with the aim of bringing about major changes in railway culture. By providing a framework for process-driven, ground-level initiatives it focused particularly strongly on empowerment and teamwork. Brian Burdsall, Director QTP, was adamant that customer care improvements should be devised and delivered by ground level staff so that they would result in real ongoing change rather than be seen as a 'spray-on' initiative.

InterCity's continuing strength and development in the market place depended on being able to convince its managers and staff that only radical improvements in customer service would keep passenger loyalty. There can be no doubt that InterCity's customer service revolution could not have taken place without the benefit of its strong commitment to Total Quality Management allied to the successful completion of its re-organisation. Under this, station and on-train staff came to work together, providing a much more focused customer service approach. From 1990 onwards, the business emphasis began to move away from the provision of new hardware towards strongly identified people initiatives.

The unseen heroes, drivers Jim White and Phillip Ford, prepare to take the new IC225 north to Edinburgh on 28th June 1991

The InterCity Ambassador

Introduction of Senior Conductors

A second major break with the past had occurred in 1989 with the introduction of the 'Senior Conductor' role. The traditional Guard's responsibilities were primarily based around revenue protection and safety. They did not work exclusively for InterCity and they could be handling Inter-City services one day and marshalling coal or aggregate traffic the next. Eight hundred and fifty new Senior Conductors were carefully selected. They were given new uniforms and equipment and worked with managers dedicated to helping them fulfil the requirements of their new role.

All Senior Conductors attended specially designed programmes to prepare them for the greater responsibility and freedom of action which they now enjoyed. For example, if a train was badly delayed, the Senior Conductor could authorise complimentary drinks or refreshments for customers. Where appropriate they were empowered to organise taxis to get passengers to their ultimate destinations if the situation warranted such action. These additional responsibilities motivated staff and were much welcomed by customers. The length of time it took to achieve this cultral change should not be under estimated.

In the past, guards tended to sit out of sight in guards' vans. They were trained to respond to operating incidents rather than to be particularly concerned about passenger needs. The new ambassadors for the business were selected from a traditional pool of Guards but the selection process ensured that those most dedicated to meeting customer requirements were chosen. One of the biggest breakthroughs in their development came when senior managers started to listen to the problems that new Senior Conductors had to face every day. They felt, for example, that once their trains were on the move that they were totally isolated from key decision makers on the ground. Often, they felt powerless and embarrassed that they could not help their customers more.

The 150 year old problem of train staff being cut off from train service Control was solved by the end of 1993. InterCity provided the Senior Conductors with bleepers and radio phones and set up shore-based Customer Service Controls. The Senior Conductor now had up-to-the-minute information on what was happening and was able to pass particular customer problems back to Control for resolution. This initiative cost less than one day's income to implement but it completely transformed the Senior Conductors' ability to seize the initiative in serving their customers. The Senior Conductor had become the ambassador for InterCity and the champion for the customer.

Delighting the customer

On his arrival in 1992, Chris Green stressed the clear hierarchy of customer needs (see below). Working from the base of the triangle, safety and reliability remained the foundation stones of passenger requirements. Only when an organisation had fully addressed these needs could it then move on to the higher consumer needs of cleanliness, information and customer service. InterCity was beginning to perform well at the basic needs level and was ready to develop the equally difficult higher needs. Senior managers dared to talk about 'delighting the customer' as the ultimate pinnacle of the customer needs' triangle.

In 1991 market research had identified InterCity as being a good product but one which had inconsistent presentation. In order to meet this challenge, the business

Model for 'delighting the customer': the hierarchy of customer needs

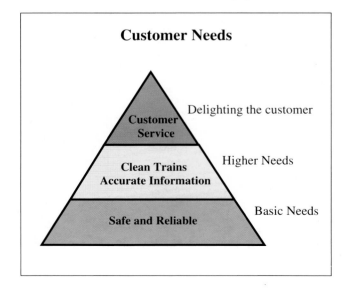

decided to bring in external expertise in customer service and appointed Graham Smith, formerly British Airways General Manager for Scotland. He proved to be a lively and creative crusader for the consumer and played a strong role in a new Customer Service Council. This was made up from a complete cross-section of individuals throughout InterCity from members of Directors' Group to station retail and depot engineering staff. The in-house enthusiasm, energy and experience of staff was channelled through a number of seminars to solve many of InterCity's own problems in an approach strongly influenced by the team-based QTP process.

The Trail to the Train
The in-house work developed 'The Trail to the Train' concept which helped to identify difficulties encountered by customers while travelling by InterCity. These difficulties needed to be removed. A number of exciting solutions were found for problems encountered at each of the stages and the degree of success was tracked through three-monthly customer opinion polls conducted by external market research professionals. These picked up the strengths and weaknesses that were of concern to customers. The research enabled the business to track the 'Quality Gap' between the level of importance customers attached to a certain service and the levels of satisfaction they were receiving from that service.

By early 1994 it was clear that InterCity was well on the way to meeting many more of its customers' needs. This was undoubtedly due to the hard work and enterprise of the dedicated teams that had worked on the problems identified in 'The Trail to the Train' and their achievements are best explained through a number of examples.

An extract from the Customer Service research carried out in Autumn 1993

CUSTOMER SATISFACTION

	Satisfactory %	Excellent %
Courtesy of Senior Conductors	97	74
Cleanliness of trains	92	67
Courtesy of station staff	90	59
Information on stations	90	62
Cleanliness of stations	88	50
Queuing time for tickets	85	57

INTERCITY

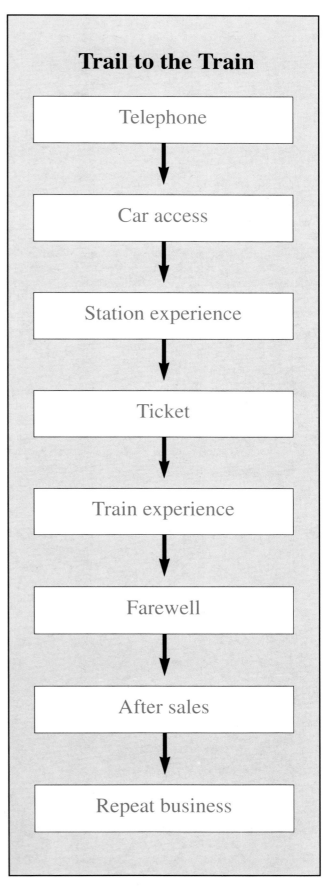

Trail to the Train

Telephone

↓

Car access

↓

Station experience

↓

Ticket

↓

Train experience

↓

Farewell

↓

After sales

↓

Repeat business

Telephone Enquiries

The first point of contact with the customer was of vital importance. Increasingly, customers expected to do business by telephone. In 1993 InterCity answered 1,800,000 phone calls a month – on average one call per second for the two shifts available. Detailed analysis revealed that a better and more consistent standard of service could be offered through larger Telephone Enquiry Bureaux (TEB) and so the total number of TEB was therefore rationalised to a total of twenty across the UK. Significantly greater use was made of part-time staff and of computerised timetables and telephone answering equipment.

The new enquiry offices were still labour-intensive and telephone operators were often required to respond to 25 calls per hour throughout their shift. The future lay in operators answering less calls but converting more of those calls into a sale. Thereafter the trend was towards new telesales offices equipped to answer enquiries, issue tickets and make reservations. Recorded tapes increasingly helped to answer routine enquiries.

Car Parks

InterCity will never increase its market share without being able to welcome the car to the station. In the 1990s much scarce investment was diverted into providing extra car parking at motorway 'Gateway' stations such as Luton, Watford, Reading and Stevenage. Increasing attention was also paid to the security of cars which were often left unattended for long periods. In 1993 InterCity adopted the new AA Silver and Gold Secure car park standards and this involved further investment in CCTV surveillance, better lighting and more patrols.

Customers need easy access to trains; enlarged car parks are a principal feature of Gateway stations

A smiling Porter welcomes customers at Kings Cross

Porters

InterCity customers arriving at stations with luggage wanted porters – however inconvenient this may have been to railway managers. In 1993 a logical way was found to re-introduce the porter in a stylish manner. The solution was to recruit additional staff to provide a quality porterage service for a fixed fee of two pounds. Their distinctive uniforms and friendly approach provided an additional welcome at a growing number of InterCity stations. The initial experiment, carried out at King's Cross, won spectacular headlines and articles in the media and a warm response from long distance customers. The scheme was extended to other major InterCity stations and ranked as a real victory for customer service.

Telesales

The point of maximum customer stress occurred in the ticket queue just before departure. The customer-friendly solution did not lie in providing still more ticket windows. It emerged that the best way to book a ticket was to avoid the ticket office all together.

Many customers actually wanted to buy their tickets from the peace and quiet of their own home or from the convenience of their own office. This had been achieved in a pilot exercise carried out at Reading which was so successful that it led to the immediate investment in a £2m Telesales office in Newcastle. This opened in November 1993 and was staffed by a team of highly motivated, committed people. Customers phoned 0800 450 450, quoted their credit card numbers, discussed the journey opportunities and then received their tickets by first class mail.

The successful move to Telesales could not have been accomplished without significant investment in new ticketing issuing machines. InterCity, in association with European Passenger Services, had invested nearly £17m in a new ticketing system called Tribute. This gave travel packages which, combined with telesales, provided a state-of-the-art purchasing system.

Zoning of platforms helps customers locate the correct coach

Customer Welcome

One point that was raised at the Customer Service Council was the tremendous difference in the initial reception customers encountered when they first made use of an airline as opposed to InterCity. Railways have always prided themselves on letting customers process themselves through a station, but airlines put their most presentable and customer-friendly staff up-front to greet and guide arriving customers.

The idea emerged of highly visible Welcome teams on the concourses of major stations. Over 90% of InterCity customers passed through just twenty stations, and by monitoring these stations InterCity very quickly gained a good deal of evidence about the worth of this particular initiative.

Within six months, the business had established excellent training programmes and had selected well-qualified teams for all the major stations. Individuals were selected because they wanted to work in a close customer environment and came from both outside and within the railway industry. They gave InterCity a warm heart and achieved a more positive customer response than any other initiative. Their bright claret uniforms were synonymous with friendly customer service at stressful points on customers' journeys.

Platform Zoning

Unlike European countries, Britain had never been particularly good at identifying the formation of trains to passengers waiting for them to arrive.

This proved to be another stress point for customers

and in 1994 a system of dividing the platform areas into zones was taken as best practice from German railways. January 1994 saw the start of the installation of illuminated colour cubes on InterCity platforms showing a Gold Zone for First Class passengers, and blue and purple zones for Standard. Station Welcome teams, public address and special posters then advised customers where to stand for their specific coach. The best consumer ideas were often the simplest.

Train Environment

InterCity had a dedicated team of fleet engineers who worked around the clock, seven days a week, to keep the trains safe and reliable. The challenge was to get them to spread the focus of their attention from the technically exciting engine rooms and inspection pits to include the customer environment inside the train.

The change was achieved in a series of brainstorming conferences where engineers, customer service people and catering staff all worked together. The work started by sharing the results of local customer opinion surveys with the staff. These showed general satisfaction with InterCity reliability but dissatisfaction with attention to detail over internal matters within the coach such as air-conditioning, payphones, headrests, lights, interior door failures and, above all, the defects in catering equipment. All of these missing details resulted in a loss of customer support however punctual the train might be.

Each depot then went away to find its own solutions to a common problem. Some set up specialist teams; others put items out to contract and some made ingenious technical modifications. The important point was that the InterCity business had now achieved a reliable level of

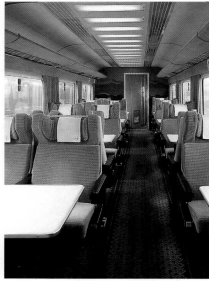

Fleet Engineers devised a programme to reduce the numbers of irritating defects to such items as internal doors, lights and toilets

Welcome host Brian Roberts in action, Euston 1993

Jane Grierson, night stewardess from Plymouth, receives her excellence award

The Silver Swallow Excellence Award

customer environment by sharing a problem and delegating the solution. Many would not have believed that a seemingly traditional part of the InterCity business could have changed so quickly. For example, better reliability in the train kitchen equipment brought an immediate return in more motivated stewards and stewardesses.

InterCity Shuttle

The InterCity Shuttle concept was introduced in May 1993 to bring all the strands of the new customer service initiatives together. Routes were selected in the high frequency, middle distance range such as Euston to the West Midlands and St Pancras to the East Midlands. These services tended to have trains with few customer or meal services but were vulnerable to Motorway competition. The principles of the shuttle service changed this and customers found:

● Welcome teams on the concourses of all principal stations served.
● Dedicated Shuttle desks provided as 'check-in' points.
● Ticket checks were eliminated at the barriers whilst the on-train team provided a trainside welcome.
● Trains were platformed and available at least 20 minutes before departure.
● Buffet cars open when they joined the train and stayed open throughout the journey and the turnround.
● Catering trolleys moved up and down both Standard and First Class throughout the journey.

Silver Swallows

It is always a problem in a large industry to say thank you to the unsung heroes and heroines who keep the railway running against all the odds.

InterCity hit upon the idea of awarding a Silver Swallow in the form of a lapel badge as its commendation for excellence. Around 300 were issued each year, averaging about one per cent of total staff.

Staff could be sponsored by customers, managers or supervisors and the citations certainly made humbling reading. A stewardess who rescued a customer who had fallen off a platform just as a train was running in; a driver who kept his train running despite suffering injuries from a brick thrown through his window; umpteen examples of individual kindness including driving customers home after they had missed late trains or even putting tourists up for the night.

The staff who wear the Silver Swallow are the elite of the InterCity teams and any member of staff can be nominated.

Changing the top team culture

The transformation from a top team seeking engineering solutions into a Directors' Group that wanted to make the customer the centre of all activity clearly did not happen overnight. The key was convincing a loyal but cynical workforce that top management was really committed to making change. The consumer initiatives did not begin in isolation. They resulted from long and searching debates at Directors' Group over the strategic direction that InterCity should take in the 1990s. This direction was eventually expressed in the form of a single vision supported by detailed strategies, group values and behaviours.

To have any chance of bringing about lasting change, the InterCity Directors' Group had to forge a clear vision of its own. It had to be seen to be pursuing courses of action that were demonstrably different in behavioural terms from the old railway whilst, at the same time, delivering the service levels and bottom line requirements of the new railway.

Given that all members bar three of Directors' group were from a railway background, it was clear that some difficult changes and choices would have to be made. Barry Woledge joined from British Airways as human Resources' Director and provided vital experience of the major cultural changes achieved in other large organisations. This gave a real purpose and structure to the change management process.

Vision, Strategy and Values

InterCity formulated the Vision, Strategy and Values which were to become the cornerstone of cultural change during the 1990s through a series of residential development sessions. The VSV as they became known, were tested at a conference where InterCity's senior executives were asked to feed back their comments. Questions raised from this conference led Directors' Group to create an Empowerment Group to look at the whole issue in more detail and from that process the InterCity 'Behaviours' were born.

Public expressions of change

Making the Vision, Strategy, Values and the Behaviours live so that they actually became part of people's way of behaving was vital to the success of InterCity. Directors had to show their commitment as role models to staff and both the VSV and the Behaviours were widely distributed throughout InterCity. A group of staff from all levels of the organisation was encouraged to develop guidelines for railway managers, concerning the help and support that they could give to on-train staff in the course of severe delays or other emergencies. Actions ranged from manning telephones to commandeering managers' mobile telephones for customers to use throughout the train. InterCity was not only seeing things differently from other organisations – it was actually behaving differently as well. If a transformation was to happen, then a culture change on that scale had to be demonstrated from the top.

Empowering for results

It was always recognised that empowerment brought additional accountability. To this end leadership style changed to fit the new values. Key financial issues such as the management of profit and loss accounts were devolved

to the routes. In turn, routes and functions were asked to manage cost, revenue targets, safety and Passenger's Charter targets. InterCity HQ had to let go by delegating but not by dumping.

In addition, the individual performance management methods used by InterCity were radically altered. A new approach was taken which ensured that the personal performances of leaders and managers were measured against hard objectives. In addition, the behaviours needed to sustain a successful customer service business, the 'how' of the job, were also closely identified and developed so that the business could be sure that not only were managers performing well but they were also behaving well both towards customers and staff.

Repeat business

The era of customer service development was one of the toughest periods in InterCity's history but it was also a very rewarding time. Putting customer requirements first demanded a thoroughly committed and almost evangelical belief in ensuring that the business and all its people were fully aligned to adding value to every encounter between staff and customers. Satisfied customers had a tendency to become repeat customers and repeat customers made the difference between profit and loss to a highly competitive business such as InterCity.

Customer service success

Helpful staff tended to be confident and competent people in their own right. These were the very people who, in turn, secured satisfied customers in their daily encounters. Nevertheless, however satisfied and able the staff, they too needed support and they needed to have their difficulties acknowledged. They also needed to know that help was there when they wanted it, especially if they were in the front-line of customer service day in and day out. In a service business, 'service' and 'business' should not be separated. It was not by chance that profit rose strongly in the 1993 recession just as InterCity got its customer service right. Consistent and clearly-defined standards were essential to an InterCity brand under extreme competitive pressure.

As a learning organisation, the key lessons for InterCity were that leadership objectives had to be aligned to excellent customer service and that senior managers had to role model their commitment. By 1994 InterCity had come to stand for a series of business principles:

- High speed passenger rail businesses must be market-led and customer driven.
- Operations and Production are clearly vital to the efficient and safe running of a railway but they must be subordinate to the customer and the market if they are to survive.
- Customer needs have to be thoroughly understood and acted upon by all staff.
- Good customer service is a key concern for all those who work for InterCity.
- Consistent standards of customer service are essential to a national brand under pressure from competition.
- Giving customers added value is paramount for repeat business.

By the early 1990s giving 'added value' to all staff and customer encounters had started to become an integral part of the InterCity business culture. There is no doubt that the cold realities of the deep recession from 1990 to 1994 forced InterCity to face up to a radical improvement in its customer service. In the strong economy of the 1980s energies had been diverted to investment in physical assets. In the insecure 1990s, the challenge of survival in the market place and the uncertainties of privatisation forced InterCity to divert energies back to investment in people. Customers service may not be one hundred per cent perfect as yet, but a large industry has discovered the will to delight its customers.

On Board Services has always been an integral part of the train team. This crew , posed at Kings Cross, wears the uniform style of 1988-1993

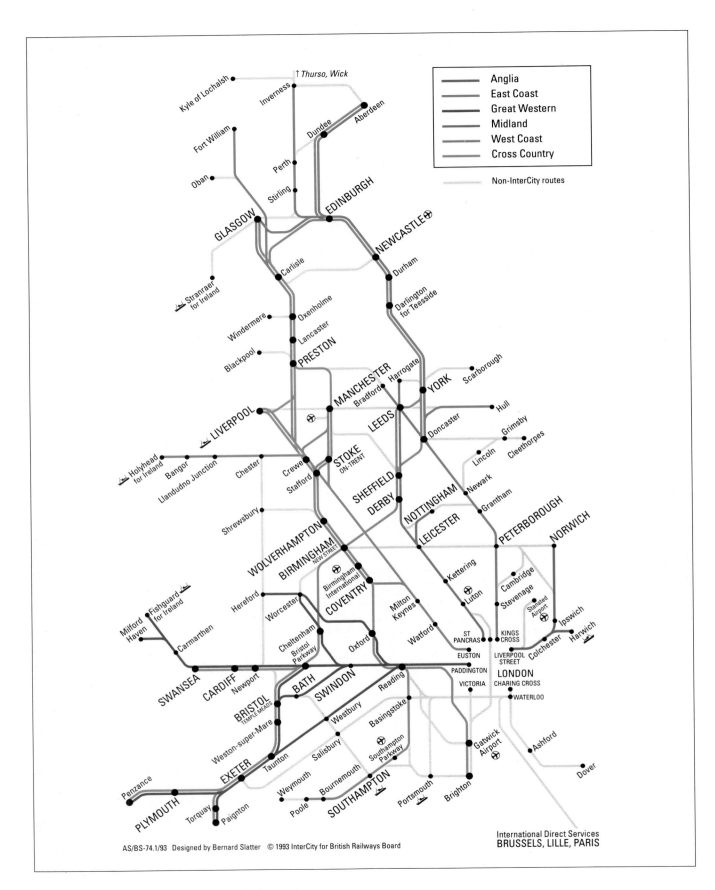

InterCity; Route by Route with associated feeder services

Chapter Nine
THE FUTURE OF INTERCITY 1994 AND BEYOND

The train of the future: the 160 mph IC250 is designed and ready

A change in organisation and ownership does not mean that InterCity's vision for the future has changed. The existing InterCity vision will almost certainly stand the test of time for this famous railway business. The future just has to be about becoming "the best, most civilised way to travel at speed from centre to centre."

The two key words that will really decide InterCity's future are 'civilised' and 'speed'. InterCity's unique selling point will quite clearly continue to be the opportunity that it offers for travellers to relax whilst travelling at speed. Everyone enjoys relaxing over the Great British Breakfast whilst reading a newspaper and cruising at 125 mph. No other form of transport has the potential to make travel so enjoyable.

A look into the future must, therefore, be concerned with three factors. Firstly, whether InterCity can survive the organisational upheaval of the 1993 Railways Act; secondly, whether InterCity can maintain a competitive speed advantage for new markets and thirdly, whether it can find its destiny as a true surface airline delivering ever higher standards of customer service.

Making reorganisation succeed
Any look into the future of InterCity must begin with the shock wave of railway privatisation in the early 1990s. This will radically change both the nature and future of the railway. The new Railways Act began to take effect from April 1994 and represented the largest reorganisation of

INTERCITY ORGANISATION

a) Unified Business 1992-94

Managing Director
Chris Green

Route Directors | HQ Directors

Anglia & Gatwick
Andy Cooper

East Coast
Brian Burdsall

Great Western
Brian Scott

Midland Cross Country
Richard Brown

West Coast
Ivor Warburton

Finance
Geoff Ashton

Fleet
Brian Clementson

Human Resources
Barry Woledge

Infrastructure
John Elliot

Marketing
John Cimelli

On Board Services
Terry Coyle

INTERCITY ORGANISATION

b) Preparation towards privatisation

Individual Train Companies

Anglia
Andy Cooper

Cross Country
Chris Tibbits

East Coast
Brian Burdsall

Great Western
Brian Scott

Midland Mainline
Richard Brown

West Coast
Ivor Warburton

Other

Marketing Services
John Cimelli

On Board Supply
Terry Coyle

Gatwick Express
Rob Mason
(no longer branded InterCity)

Other InterCity people dispersed to:-
Railtrack HQ and zones (10)
BR Infrastructure HQ and Supply Companies (14)
Rolling Stock Companies (3)
Technical Support Companies (3)
Franchise Director; Regulator; Health & Safety

Britain's railways since 1948. It brought to a premature end the most successful organisation that the railways had enjoyed since nationalisation. It had been achieved through the unified business structure called *Organising for Quality* and it ended a decade of fragmented and divisive management under the conflicting fiefdoms of General Managers, Functional Directors and Business Managers.

InterCity had briefly become a fully-fledged business from 1992 and it was able to create a vibrant commercial culture with considerable delegation of authority. From 1992 to 1994, InterCity used this business structure well to deliver dramatic improvements in both train performance and customer service on all routes.

InterCity's profit increased in 1993/94 to £100 million in spite of a severe economic recession. This was largely achieved through a company commitment to 'profit with quality' which inspired record productivity initiatives at ground level without damaging customer service. The success of the *Organising for Quality* structure lay in its delivery. The unity of a natural business structure minimised friction and maximised delivery. A powerful

team focus on delivery ran through the organisation and the notoriously difficult area of train performance saw continuous improvement for a year with the delivery of the 90% target for the first time in 1993.

Preparations for privatisation required an enormous change of direction for InterCity and were a major challenge for its leadership. Two years had been spent welding some 30,000 staff into a united force fighting for the InterCity vision. The ultimate challenge was how to retain this energy whilst re-organising yet again into much smaller units.

On 5th November 1993, the 133 clauses of the 1993 Railways Act finally became law following rowdy scenes in both the House of Commons and the House of Lords. The Act effectively broke up InterCity as a unified business and left the customer with only the original marketing brand name as a reminder of a previous era. From April 1994, the InterCity business was fragmented both vertically and horizontally. It surrendered the vertical integration of its infrastructure in the form of track, signalling and structures to the new Railtrack organisation with its ten geographical zones. It was also fragmented

Whoever operates their trains in the future, customers will expect ever-improving speeds and standards of service and comfort

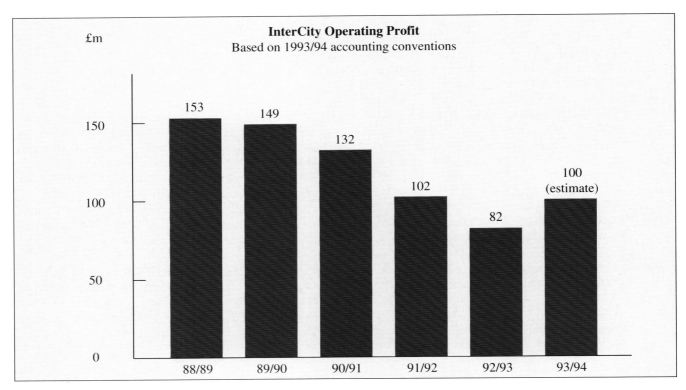

InterCity Operating Profit
Based on 1993/94 accounting conventions

£m

153 — 88/89
149 — 89/90
132 — 90/91
102 — 91/92
82 — 92/93
100 (estimate) — 93/94

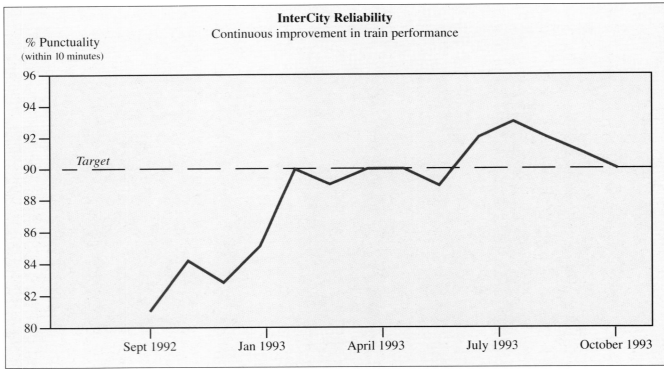

InterCity Reliability
Continuous improvement in train performance

% Punctuality
(within 10 minutes)

Target

Sept 1992   Jan 1993   April 1993   July 1993   October 1993

horizontally with the elimination of the strategic business headquarters and the break-up of its five individual routes into six train operating companies for potential franchising. This was a watershed, since virtually all railways in the world had both owned their own track and had operated their own trains since the Liverpool & Manchester Railway opened in 1830.

October 1993: Gatwick Express/Anglia
The future is clearly going to centre around the development of the six independent train companies and their attitude to the InterCity brand. The seventh train company, Gatwick Express, was recognised as the exception to the rule and effectively dropped out of the InterCity brand from 10th October 1993, when it became the first shadow franchise.

Gatwick Express was a simpler name to promote to visitors from abroad and the route was a short specialist service untypical of InterCity generally. Rob Mason became its first director and faced the challenge of daily competition against the far larger number of Network SouthEast services that duplicated his route to Gatwick Airport. Survival will depend on offering a quality alternative to the lower-priced NSE network.

At Liverpool Street, Andy Cooper remained with the Anglia train operating company from October 1993. Anglia was unique in that it was able to add the local trains in the Norwich area to its portfolio with all the advantages that this brought in terms of an integrated approach to marketing and performance. The new Anglia, like all the remaining routes, is likely to stay within the InterCity brand in the future and will develop its potential as a quality train company for East Anglia as a whole rather than just the London to Norwich corridor.

April 1994: the larger routes

The Midland Cross Country profit centre which had mirrored the old Midland Railway Company was broken into two train companies in April 1994. Midland Mainline remained based at Derby and was led by Richard Brown, whilst Cross Country set itself up as a new company in Birmingham under Chris Tibbits, a leader well-experienced in complex planning. The East Coast at York under Brian Burdsall, and the Great Western at Swindon under Brian Scott were the other InterCity routes to become shadow franchises in April, while the West Coast, led by Ivor Warburton at Birmingham completed the break up to six independent train operating companies. They reported to the residual British Rail structure but enjoyed a growing autonomy in preparation for the franchising process.

These train companies will have the choice of co-operating to retain an express network or retiring into their shells to the advantage of the competing national coach and air networks. It is likely that the train companies will hunt together for brand marketing but will diverge for the entrepreneurial tasks such as customer service and labour relations. Confident management teams will see the benefit of promoting network travel to the benefit of rail's modal share of the market.

In 1993 the InterCity team won three significant victories which will shape and strengthen the future of the InterCity brand. On 4th November 1993 the Board was persuaded to support the retention of the InterCity brand despite the break-up of the organisation that had created and developed it. The InterCity brand was a trade mark of the Board and it was to be retained and promoted as an endorsement brand for the six train companies which now operate the fast centre-to-centre services.

Secondly, a new Marketing Services organisation led by John Cimelli was also agreed on the same date to manage the brand on behalf of the train companies as well as to co-ordinate joint products such as Railcards, sales teams and advertising. Whatever the future holds for InterCity, it is now certain that the famous name will continue as the brand label for fast, civilised rail transport in Britain. The mechanism for joint marketing has now been provided and the challenge will be to see how far each train company can maintain a sense of InterCity networking, whilst at the same time, supplying some of its own individual style to the delivery of customer service.

Anglia train company in action – a Norwich to London service near Manningtree

The third victory was the retention of the On Board Services (OBS) organisation for the supply of high quality train catering services. The dramatic improvements in train catering that took place over the period from 1988 to 1993 were the result of the new OBS organisation which brought a high level of attention to detail in the selection and training of an enthusiastic young staff, together with the preparation of new menus and the provision of trolley services. From April 1994 On Board Services became OBS Company and concentrated on the management of the complex shorebases together with the procurement and supply of food, whilst the train companies served the food much as an airline. OBS Company is likely to face a trade sale in the mid 1990s and the future will hold a lot of excitement in the development of new ideas for on-train catering as the train companies begin to differentiate their products.

The success of the 1994 reorganisation will ultimately hinge on its ability to deliver new sources of investment funding for the railway industry. The nationalisation era 1948-1994 brought feasts and famines of investment depending on the state of the national exchequer. The overall result was a long-term under-investment in the railway and InterCity, in particular, was unable to achieve its full potential. The privatisation era from 1994 will have succeeded if it can deliver consistent investment to an industry with long payback periods and benefits which are often as much socio-economic as they are commercial.

The quest for speed

The second strategic challenge in the future must be the quest for higher speed. InterCity faces unregulated competition from airlines, coaches, company cars, private cars and toll-free motorways, on a scale unknown in the rest of Europe. It must therefore continue its remorseless battle to travel faster between centres. It seems probable that the UK's quest for speed will have to take place on existing tracks rather than on brand new, purpose-built railways. Britain is most unlikely to build a major new railway through its industrial heartland. Were it to do so, that line would undoubtedly connect Manchester, Birmingham, London and the Channel Tunnel with a 200mph (320km/h) Very High Speed passenger link offering radical improvements in journey times such as Manchester to London in less than one and a half hours. The London to Folkestone link, now known as Union Railways, is however, the only part of the route that is likely to be built.

The need for high speed routes will be a red hot issue for years to come

The extensive InterCity Strategy Review of 1989 was unable to establish any financial case for a new railway between London and Manchester. World-wide comparisons gave the reasons why Britain was unlikely to need or to build a new north/south railway in the next century. Japan and France, for example, were able to call on huge passenger volumes for their new railways which are just not available in the UK, due to the shorter distances involved and the diversification of the routes. As a rule of thumb, it does seem that a new railway needs a minimum usage of about 20 million journeys per annum, together with a willingness on the customer's part to pay a significant premium for very high speed.

Studies carried out in 1989 also showed a strong resistance to premium fares for speed in the UK and the expected revenue from any new line would have fallen short by a factor of three. The case remained stubbornly negative even if other destinations on the West Coast were included, whilst demand was far below the levels achieved on the Paris to Lyons route.

From these studies emerged the InterCity vision to develop the existing main routes for 160mph operation over the next decades. This can be achieved by harnessing modern technology to extract even more value from existing tracks. A package of developments was put in hand to ensure that 160mph operation was deliverable by the end of the century. The key feature was the development of the InterCity 250 train. This 25kV electric push-pull train was originally designed to operate on the West Coast but would also be ideal for the well-aligned routes out of Kings Cross and Paddington. It was put out to tender in 1992 for the West Coast, but is now waiting in the wings for funding. It is to be hoped that the new rolling stock companies will seize the opportunity that the InterCity 250 offers for an early investment in speed and comfort.

Plugging InterCity into Europe

One of the most exciting new markets for InterCity must lie in the opening of the Channel Tunnel in mid-1994. The direct Eurostar services to Paris and Brussels are operated by a sister company, European Passenger Services, but there are considerable opportunities for all UK rail operators.

Paris is some 250 miles from London and therefore lies within the ideal threshold of three hour rail journeys. The separation of Britain from Europe by the Channel gave air most of the market by the 1980s but this will be dramatically reversed in the 1990s. A flood of visitors will now arrive in the centre of London by rail instead of by air and they will be far more likely to continue their onward journey by rail. InterCity gains as the diversity of destinations from London limits the case for numerous through international trains to the north and west. There will be two sleeper trains and five day trains from principal UK regional centres direct to Paris and Brussels, but InterCity will be able to complement these by offering frequent feeder services to and from the London-based Eurostar network.

This First Class mock-up of the IC250 now resides in a warehouse. The vehicles should have been in service by 1995

PLUGGING INTERCITY INTO EUROPE – DRAFT TIMETABLES

BEYOND LONDON DAY TRAINS
(All times shown are local and are 1994 draft plans)

SCOTLAND – PARIS/BRUSSELS

Glasgow Central	0515	0708	
Edinburgh	0637	0816	
Newcastle	0802	0945	
Darlington	0830	1017	
York	0901	1048	
Doncaster	0926	1113	
Newark	0950	1137	
Peterborough	1022	1209	
Lille Europe	1451		
Paris Nord		1753	
Brussels Midi	1533		

BRUSSELS/PARIS – SCOTLAND

Brussels Midi		1555	
Paris Nord	1313		
Lille Europe	1414	1635	
Peterborough	1635	1900	
Newark	1715	1929	
Doncaster	1740	1955	
York	1805	2020	
Darlington	1835	2049	
Newcastle	1905	2120	
Edinburgh	2031	2246	
Glasgow Central	2143	2355	

MANCHESTER – PARIS/BRUSSELS

Manchester Piccadilly		0608	0935
Stockport		0617	0944
Crewe		0650	1011
Stafford		0710	1031
Wolverhampton		0731	–
Birmingham New Street	0600	0752	–
Birmingham International	0611	0803	–
Coventry	0622	0816	–
Rugby	0636	0826	1109
Milton Keynes Central	0701	0847	1134
Lille Europe		1251	
Paris Nord	1156		1623
Brussels Midi		1331	

BRUSSELS/PARIS – MANCHESTER

Brussels Midi	1735		
Paris Nord		1743	1928
Lille Europe	1815		2032
Milton Keynes Central	1954	2024	2223
Rugby	2019	2051	2249
Coventry	2032	–	2301
Birmingham International	2043	–	2312
Birmingham New Street	2057	–	2326
Wolverhampton	2117	–	
Stafford	2135	2128	
Crewe	2202	2153	
Stockport	2230	2220	
Manchester Piccadilly	2240	2230	

Map of Eurostar Full Day Service,
European Passenger Services

BEYOND LONDON NIGHT TRAINS
(All times shown are local and are 1994 draft plans)

GLASGOW – PARIS/BRUSSELS

Glasgow Central	1808
Carlisle	1931
Lancaster	2029
Preston	2054
Crewe	2139
Paris Nord	0705
Brussels Midi	0820

PARIS/BRUSSELS – GLASGOW

Brussels Midi	2224
Paris Nord	2214
Crewe	0700
Preston	0755
Lancaster	0815
Carlisle	0914
Glasgow Central	1040

PLYMOUTH – BRUSSELS

Plymouth	1950
Newton Abbot	2030
Exeter	2055
Taunton	2124
Bristol Temple Meads	2210
Bath	2224
Swindon	2254
Brussels Midi	0820

BRUSSELS – PLYMOUTH

Brussels Midi	2224
Swindon	0510
Bath	0545
Bristol Temple Meads	0610
Taunton	0655
Exeter	0727
Newton Abbot	0750
Plymouth	0835

SOUTH WALES – PARIS

Swansea	1915
Cardiff	2020
Newport	2040
Bristol Temple Meads	2142
Bath	2156
Swindon	2213
Paris Nord	0705

PARIS – SOUTH WALES

Paris Nord	2214
Swindon	0525
Bath	0605
Bristol Temple Meads	0700
Newport	0726
Cardiff	0743
Swansea	0835

A Eurostar train on test in France

The scale of marketing opportunities for UK-based rail operators is immense. An estimated 47 million air trips are made annually to and from mainland Europe and many short-hop transits will be ideally suited to the rail mode compared with the existing rail and sea journey of around six hours.

There is little doubt that the three hour Eurostar journeys direct to Paris and Brussels will take at least half the existing air market. The InterCity network naturally feeds into London and strong joint advertising will promote the new European rail market and will bring important new feeder travel onto the InterCity network. Flexibility will be the order of the day. A passenger from York, for example, may choose to travel by the direct Eurostar train to Paris but could return using InterCity East Coast from London to York.

The through trains north of London from 1995 will offer daytime connections with InterCity services at seventeen stations and night services at a further fifteen. The day Eurostar trains are likely to appeal to the leisure customer but the sleepers offer a good chance of attracting new business travellers on journeys such as Glasgow to Paris or Plymouth to Brussels.

£800m has been invested in the modernisation of existing routes to the Channel Tunnel which will bring benefits to thousands of domestic rail customers. Brand new, state-of-the-art Eurostars will take their place alongside stylish InterCity trains locking the United Kingdom into the growing European high-speed network of railways. Train journeys to Paris and Brussels will be commonplace during this decade with the promise of exciting destinations such as Madrid, Milan and Munich on the horizon. The Channel Tunnel will bring the railways of Britain and Europe closer together and this should bring a healthy interchange of technical developments which has been long overdue.

Union Railways

This is not the end of the impact of Europe on the future UK rail passenger network, however. The success of the newly constructed 180mph railways in France, Germany and Spain may yet lead to a similar development in UK high speed rail construction. It is already clear that rail's potential to and from mainland Europe will become restrained by the demands on the existing route from Waterloo to Folkestone around the turn of the century. Eurostar will make the construction of the £3 billion Union Railways route inevitable if Britain wishes to retain an efficient link to mainland Europe. The proposal will offer high-speed operation on a brand new track alignment through some of the most congested parts of the south east. Customers will gain a dramatic 35 minute journey from St Pancras to the Channel Tunnel instead of Eurostar's 60 minute journey along its previous route.

The new line is currently being planned in detail for a Parliamentary decision around 1996. It will offer the opportunity to continue the excellent TGV Nord to the Thames and will enable the latest technology to be used in signalling, cab control, electrification and train design. It will bring Paris within 2 hours 30 minutes of London, less than today's journey time from London to Manchester. Most importantly, it will make St Pancras/ Kings Cross an international crossroads feeding directly into the East Coast, the East Midlands, the West Coast (perhaps via a people mover) and Thameslink – not to mention five Underground lines.

Faster on existing railways

On the domestic scene, it is clear both from the work of institutions such as the Henley Centre and from InterCity's own market research that a series of major transport mis-matches will occur by the end of the century. InterCity's central objective was the promotion of major investment in the modernisation of its infrastructure and trains to achieve an advantage over its air and road competitors. This was built around taking one major route each decade and totally renewing all the assets and trains to create a step change in speed and reliability.

The East Coast was a highly successful first step in the 1980s. The intention was to follow on with the West Coast in the 1990s and the Great Western in the period 2000/2010, together with the other HST routes such as Midland and Cross Country. This cycle was unfortunately broken by the drying-up of investment funds as the recession bit from 1991.

There must now be real concern that postponing the decade-by-decade investment vision has only served to delay the inevitable. Both the comprehensive West Coast and the Great Western modernisation schemes may now have to be carried out simultaneously rather than in an orderly sequence as originally planned. Funding permitting, the future holds an exciting potential for main line modernisation, upgrading and acceleration as the following case studies show. This will provide a positive opportunity for rail privatisation to demonstrate its undoubted advantage in bringing new sources of funding to the table.

APT demonstrates its ability to 'lean into' curves, so permitting higher speeds on existing current tracks

Tilting technology for higher speeds already exists in Sweden where the X2000 is now in service

CASE STUDY: WEST COAST 1995-2005 AD

A major £800m modernisation plan has been developed which will allow conventional trains to travel at 125mph from London to Coventry and Crewe. Initially, this would be introduced at the southern end of the route but could be accelerated northwards, as funds became available.

Half of the spending will be on infrastructure – the signalling and electrification systems, mostly 30 years old or more, need renewal and new track layouts will allow increased speeds in key locations.

Complementing this, new trains will be needed as the existing locomotives are limited to 110mph. Options include the InterCity 225 (as on the East Coast) or the new InterCity 250 which was fully designed and tendered in 1992 but which is now frozen awaiting funding.

Looking into the next century, potential will still exist for tilt trains to exploit the new track alignments even further to 160mph and proven tilt trains are now operating in both Italy and Sweden. This would be of special interest for London to Glasgow services where a tilt train could get close to the Holy Grail of a four hour journey time.

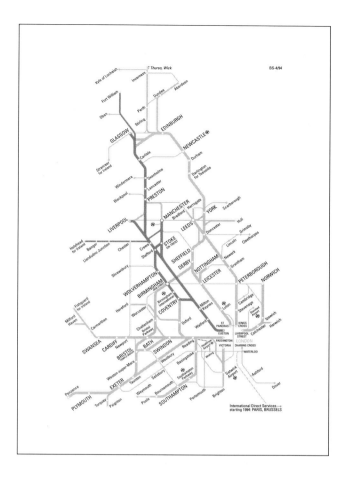

West Coast expresses are limited to 110mph pending route modernisation

CASE STUDY: GREAT WESTERN 2000-2010 AD

The Great Western currently offers the fastest diesel timetable in the world using 125mph HSTs on a very straight and well-aligned railway. These diesels fall due for renewal at the turn of the century and this will offer an exciting strategic opportunity for a major step change.

The vision would be to accelerate the existing route to 160mph by exploiting the straight and level nature of Brunel's track and then to continue the Heathrow electrification beyond Hayes to Bristol and Swansea. Selective track re-alignment would be needed and, as the entire route is due for resignalling in the same time period, full cab signalling could be introduced at the same time to enhance the existing automatic train protection.

This would produce a showpiece railway for the UK with a journey time from London to Cardiff of just 80 minutes compared with the existing two hours.

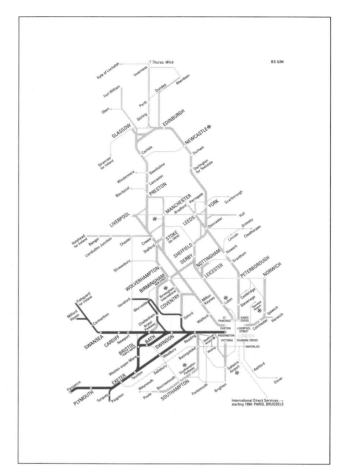

The whole Great Western HST fleet is due for renewal around the year 2000

132

CASE STUDY: MIDLAND MAIN LINE, CROSS COUNTRY, ANGLIA 2000-2010 AD

These three routes have tended to depend on InterCity's cascading strategy in the past, as justification for re-equipment was always easier on the big earning routes such as the East Coast.

The HSTs and the Class 47s of Midland main line and Cross Country will need replacing by the turn of the century. This will provide a once-in-a-generation opportunity to justify the extension of electrification from Bedford to Sheffield via Derby, with a route to Nottingham. A cascade of IC225s from the East Coast, or more adventurously an electric tilt train, could bring dramatic speed improvements in the route's battle with the M1. In 1975 the APT tilt train demonstrated a 58 minute journey time between London and Leicester.

Cross Country faces the choice of fill-in electrification between Bristol and York, life extension of cascaded HSTs or a new design of diesel locomotive in the next century. It seems possible that fill-in electrification will be selected for the central core of Cross Country with diesel haulage beyond the wires at the peripheries.

Gatwick is already looking at an upgraded Networker 365/3 for a high performance, low cost replacement in the 1990s and it is possible that Anglia would wish to do something similar once this versatile dual voltage train has been fully commissioned.

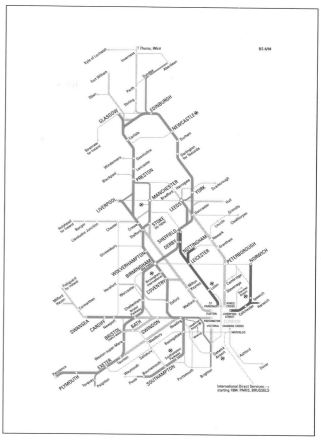

The Midland main line from St Pancras was electrified for Network South East services to Bedford. IC125s already run 'under the wires' for nearly one-third of their journeys

CASE STUDY: EAST COAST 2010-2020 AD

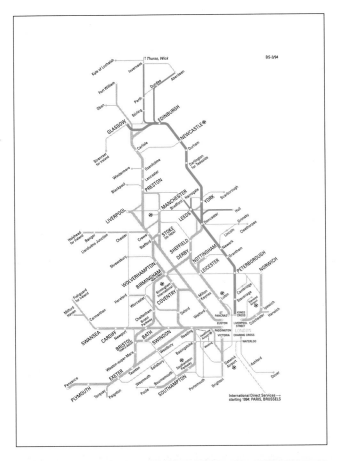

The 125mph East Coast is potentially a 160mph, high speed railway already south of Darlington and initial planning suggests that a £1 billion investment would be needed to straighten out the whole route for virtually continuous 160mph running between London and Newcastle. This could offer a three and a half hour journey time from London to Edinburgh without the need for tilting trains.

As a first stage, the present 125mph operation can be stepped up to 140mph with the existing Class 91 electric locomotives as soon as cab signalling and various other lineside features are provided. Thereafter, it is a question of a series of track re-alignments, a new tunnel under York station and a diversion line in the Newcastle area if the full 160mph potential is to be realised.

The results outlined above, however, are dramatic enough to make the construction of a new railway unnecessary and would be very similar to the use of TGVs on existing tracks south of Tours. The investment could also bring a TGV-type impact on the domestic air services between London, Newcastle and Edinburgh.

This aerial view of York shows how a high speed route would demand a tunnel under the station area

CASE STUDY: INTERCITY SPECIAL TRAINS

InterCity Special Trains

InterCity Special Trains was set up in 1985 under the leadership of David Ward. The scope of the business ranged from operating special VIP charters and luxury weekend excursions through to responsibility for steam trains on the mainline railway; and last, but by no means least, managing the Royal Train.

The unit utilised financially written down rolling stock and has been able to demonstrate a small profit each year since its launch. Special Trains specialised in operating high quality charter services for the railway and private companies and provided traditional Pullman style service on board. Business charters were regularly run to Ascot, the Cheltenham Gold Cup and the Grand National.

The Special Trains business had been very much part of InterCity. Their coaches were some of the first to be painted in the new InterCity livery. Over the last nine years they have brought nostalgia back into rail travel together with a welcome contribution to InterCity's income despite the severe recession in the early 1990s.

A decision was taken in 1994 to offer the Special Trains' assets for sale and care will be taken to ensure that this unique activity retains an important place in the future rail industry. Its assets included six Class 47 locomotives and over 200 coaches together with contracts for the haulage of famous private trains such as the Royal Scotsman and the Venice-Simplon-Orient Express.

A Special Trains Land Cruise offers its clients spectacular Highland views

The quest for customer service

InterCity developed in the 1980s through its successes in the quest for speed. The intensive exploitation of the High Speed Train and the InterCity 225 brought a welcome boost in income, in competitive edge and in public perception. By 1990, most of the easy speed improvements had been achieved and investment was reduced to a trickle by the recession and the uncertainties of a major re-organisation. It was natural that InterCity should transfer its development in the 1990s to the equally important area of Customer Service.

The quest for speed is not the end of the story and the third and final area for future development must lie in customer service. The fastest operator can still lose customers to a slower competitor who is offering excellence in personal service. InterCity has to be not just the fastest but also the best, most civilised way to travel. In the early 1990s InterCity learnt how to start turning itself into a surface airline for both the domestic and Eurostar markets. Airlines are going to continue improving their customer service in the future and the railways will have to do the same, bearing in mind that it will have to be delivered by six separate companies working at arm's length yet, at the same time, facing similar needs.

The ultimate test for customer service: the Royal Train in InterCity hands en route to Kingswear 1992

The 1990s will see a further major development in those 'soft' areas of investment in people both because the customer will demand it and because, unlike physical investment, it can be delivered relatively quickly and evenly on all routes. It is significant that British Airways was most talked about for its leap forward in customer service delivery in the 1980s rather than the type or speed of the latest aircraft that it had introduced.

It is a safe prediction that further exciting customer developments are going to follow thick and fast as entrepreneurs develop in the new train companies. The key to success will be to find those customer service initiatives which meet a proven customer need rather than the inspirational guesses of the supplier. Research shows, for example, that there is a low demand for gimmicks such as seat-back television, as customers feel that the train window already offers a far better television picture. It does, however, point to a huge, pent-up demand for the stress to be taken out of travelling through faster ticket sales, the end of concourse queues before departure, the certainty of a seat, better real-time information, better catering and far more contact with friendly, professional staff.

The agenda for the 1990s is now becoming clear. It is to win InterCity's place as a surface airline for the UK through meeting customer needs in a really fundamental and creative way. The solutions fall into those that need

One innovation on coaches of the future will include plug-in radio and CD points at every seat

technical innovation and those that are about the quality of the individual encounters between staff and customers.

On train developments

Turning to the train, it is clear that the demand for real-time information on board is also going to force the pace of technical change. In 1993, InterCity introduced the world's first satellite-linked train to give train travellers real-time information on its location, punctuality and calling points. The train uses the same geo-stationary satellites that are employed by the US Army, to enable the train to locate itself continuously without any other lineside equipment and then gives passengers the correct visual information. This leaves the Senior Conductor free to concentrate more fully on customers' other needs. It is hoped to upgrade the whole passenger fleet over the next decade.

Tribute for faster ticketing

Technical innovation will certainly be needed in the speeding-up of ticket queues and in providing real-time information. A good place to start, therefore, would be to look at InterCity's £17m investment in a radical new ticketing system called 'Tribute'. This had been under development since 1990 and was intended to replace all existing ticket machines in booking offices and telephone enquiry bureaux. By good luck or design, it also represented the only possible means of displaying all the new fares options to customers at the point of sale. The essence of

the 1993 Railways Act is to offer the customer choice between competing products. This makes it essential to be able to display the various complex pricing offers on a screen at the booking office. None of the established ticketing systems are capable of adaption to this highly complex task.

Tribute was commissioned at St Pancras station in January 1994 and was introduced progressively across the network thereafter starting at Newcastle Telesales. No better example could be given of Tribute as a vision of the future than its application at the Telesales office. Tribute enables customers to be first talked through the timetable options, then the fare options and finally checks and debits their credit cards. Their ticket is then automatically issued and posted first class to their home address. The final step in the process is that the ticket revenue is allocated automatically to all the train companies involved and all in the space of a free customer call taking about three minutes. A future development in 1994 will enable Telesales to 'teleport' the tickets by electronic mail to a station of the customer's choice for local collection.

Self service ticketing

Not all customers can buy their tickets in advance. Many prefer a fast service at the station. They frequently ask for self-help machines which will accept credit cards without other complications. This is clearly a sensible way for regular travellers to beat the queues and in 1994 an enterprising firm offered such a machine for trial. It can issue a ticket in about 30 seconds including a credit card validity check. InterCity has already commissioned development work and a promising technical solution is

CASE STUDY: TRIBUTE

Tribute represents a major step towards airline-style ticketing on the railways. It combines a wide range of ingenious developments:

- Tribute will hold the whole UK timetable as well as the national structure of over one million fares. For the first time ever, Tribute will bring together all timetable, fares and reservations information onto one system.
- The travel ticket and the seat reservation are combined into a single boarding card which has met a real customer need.
- Travel agents throughout the world will be able to issue rail tickets on their existing terminals by accessing the Tribute system as though it was just another airline.
- Around 400 destinations in mainland Europe have been included for direct issue at UK stations on the new Tribute machines.
- European Passenger Services has adoped Tribute for both Waterloo and Ashford stations.
- Tribute will allocate the revenue from each ticket to the appropriate train companies based on a pre-agreed formula.

Easier reservations through Tribute combined with clearer seat identification in refurbished coaches will help customers find their seats on busy trains

The first Tribute ticket issuing machine was commissioned at St Pancras on 9th February 1994

INTERCITY			
STD SUPERSAVER	OUTWARD	VALID FROM	15 FEBRUARY 1994
From INVERNESS		VALID UNTIL	15 FEBRUARY 1994
To READING BR		Adult ONE	Child NIL
Route NOT LONDON			

Journey details (for codes see over)   Coach seat N/S Accom.
15FBY 07.50 INVERNESS   EDINBURGH   11.18 B 16F N SEAT
15FBY 11.45 EDINBURGH   BIRMINGHAM N ST 16.02 C 16F N SEAT
15FBY 17.06 BIRMINGHAM N ST READING   19.04 C 13F N SEAT

NOT VALID ON FRIDAYS/OTHER "PEAK" DAYS - ENQUIRE.

Issued at 3149 73 15005003 00161 09FBY94 13.30 ADULT CHEQUE £69.00   For conditions see over

The new Tribute ticket combines seat reservations with the travel document

Senior Conductors may become the Train Managers of the future

emerging which will be seen initially on the busy Shuttle routes.

Seat reservations are an important part of a relaxing journey, but everyone hates waiting on the concourse whilst hundreds of reservation labels are attached to seats. A microchip will soon enable Senior Conductors to light up the reserved seats throughout the length of a train within one minute of joining their train. InterCity will be testing other ideas for the 21st century which include computer jackpoints for laptop computers, fax machines, copiers and a technical solution to the vexing problem of making mobile phones work reliably in tunnels and cuttings.

Welcoming customers

Technology will not be the only solution to future needs and there are many areas where the 'soft' areas of people selection, training and motivation can be equally effective. The most likely area for development lies at the heart of the staff/customer encounter and will take InterCity into the quality world of 'blue-chip' hotels, restaurants and airlines. For instance, motorists arriving at major stations will come to expect a greeting on arrival at the car park entrance by a Welcome team that can help to organise not just car parking, but security, luggage assistance, ticketing and train running information, as well as other forms of assistance. The Welcome team will need to be carefully selected, well-trained and superbly supported by information systems.

Customers will be helped through the station to their train as a matter of course. They are likely to await its arrival in heated, enclosed waiting areas with a Welcome team member offering hospitality and up-to-the-minute information as well as telephone and fax services. On the train itself, customers will be recognised by their names thanks to the Tribute ticketing system and this will encourage a more personal, hotel-style service. This will also open up the opportunity for train staff to alert passengers personally just before their alighting point.

Customer service on the train will inevitably move towards the Pullman model with one attendant per coach offering a far more attentive and personalised service in First Class and, perhaps, one attendant for every two coaches in Standard. The overwhelming success of the 'Voyager' experiment on Cross Country points to the very high value that customers place on continuous personal service on a long journey.

The Senior Conductor will probably evolve into the Train Manager along the pioneering lines of European Passenger Services. The Duty Manager on every InterCity train will have total authority for train service, catering, cleaning and customer service. Customer expectations are rising rapidly and mobile train cleaners capable of refreshing InterCity's 5,000 train toilets every hour will soon be essential if the Train Manager is to meet future customer needs. Customer service is about grinding attention to detail and it is certainly going to occupy almost as much attention as investment over the next decade. Technology will not be enough – the people issues of customer service must also be delivered.

Conclusion

InterCity has made an amazing journey in its first 28 years of life from 1966 to 1994. It has transformed itself from a large subsidised industry into a marketing sector and then on to a unified business brand with a £1 billion turnover and a respectable profit. It has achieved a 94% brand awareness, equal to that of the very best high street stores, and is rated with the best airlines for customer service.

The InterCity name will continue to act as the symbol for fast, civilised rail travel in the UK. It will be more difficult to sustain and develop the brand through six fragmented train companies but the determination exists to make it work. It is hard to see how the individual train companies could take on a national airline or a national bus company without a common focus for generic advertising, promotions and public relations.

Rail has a significant advantage over its air and road competitors in that it is the only form of transport which is likely to increase journey speeds in the future. Rail can anticipate an increase in speed from 125mph to 160mph in the UK – over double the legal road limit. This will be enough to maintain a competitive advantage so long as it is coupled with ever higher standards of customer service. InterCity has learnt a major lesson: people will increasingly matter more than machines in the 1990s.

The six train companies must now carry the InterCity banner into the future along with the best wishes of all of those people who have helped InterCity to develop over the last 28 years. Their vision is likely to remain the same, to be –

> "the best, most civilised way to
> travel at speed from centre to centre."

Welcome to the routes of Britain.

INTERCITY

InterCity in the News

*On 28th June 1993, Her Majesty The Queen inaugurated
the modernised East Coast route by travelling on a special InterCity 225 train*

Before leaving London's Kings Cross station Her Majesty inspected the new electric locomotive which was to haul the inaugural train and named it 'Queen Elizabeth II'

On board the train, Her Majesty shares a moment with John Welsby, BR's Chief Executive; John Prideaux, and BRB Chairman Sir Bob Reid

On arrival in Edinburgh, Her Majesty was invited to name a second locomotive 'Palace Of Holyroodhouse' by John Prideaux, InterCity Managing Director

The Prince of Wales discusses facilities for disabled travellers in a refurbished Mark III coach in June 1985

The Queen Mother names a Class 90 locomotive 'The Girls' Brigade' at Euston station in April 1993.

As part of the occasion the Girls' Brigade National Presidents received their InterCity colours

Prime Ministerial Seals of Approval

InterCity's Director, Anglia – Andy Cooper proudly receives the prestigious Charter Mark from the Prime Minister on 27th October 1993

Harold and Mary Wilson were frequent InterCity travellers in the mid-1960s

Baroness Thatcher names an InterCity 125 'John Grooms' at Paddington

The Men from the Ministry

John MacGregor, Secretary of State for Transport, tries out the radio in InterCity's market testing vehicle in May 1993

Roger Freeman, Minister for Public Transport, joins Chris Green, Managing Director of InterCity, to try out the market testing vehicle

InterCity makes a hit with Radio One FM

Simon Bates, Radio One DJ, broadcasts live from a special train on the East Coast on 30th September 1992

InterCity provides an unusual but popular location for a recording studio

Catherine Zeta Jones names a Class 91, 'BBC Radio One FM', at Kings Cross

Simon Bates and Lulu – New recruits to InterCity?

Some Famous Naming Ceremonies with InterCity

Andrew Lloyd Webber and Stephanie Lawrence name a locomotive 'Starlight Express' at Euston station on 1st October 1984

Jimmy Savile names an HST 'Top of The Pops' at Bristol in August 1984

Mrs Jane Adley is joined by her son, Simon, and by Sir Bob Reid to commemorate her husband the late Robert Adley by naming a locomotive after him on 17th November 1993

Some of the stars of 'Emmerdale Farm' launch 'The Yorkshire Pullman' at Kings Cross in May 1988

InterCity's Special Trains for the Edinburgh Book Fair

Cyril Bleasdale helps to auction books on board the special train

Margaret Drabble takes a break on-board the special train

Terry Wogan being interviewed whilst travelling north

Family Railcard sponsored the touring production of 'Tales of Narnia' in 1991

Tim Rice with some admirers at Edinburgh Waverley station

151

INTERCITY – A FACTFILE

This InterCity Factfile is an historic record of InterCity at the peak of its 28 year development. Britain has given the InterCity name to the world for civilised, high speed travel. InterCity is proud to have spent its last six years in profit (£100 million in 1993/94) where it became Europe's only mainline railway to operate without subsidy.

The privatisation will now lead to the fragmentation of this united InterCity business into six independent train operating companies and numerous different supply and infrastructure activities.

InterCity has moved from a production-led railway into the surface airline of the UK. Managers and staff have worked with real enthusiasm to create those missing ingredients of customer welcome, quality catering, good information and clean trains and stations.

INTERCITY – THE VISION

InterCity's Vision:

"to be the best, most civilised way to travel at speed from centre to centre."

InterCity Strategy:

The strategy to achieve the vision is:

1. To focus on quality as seen by our customers and deliver a consistent, safe and relaxing service.

2. To improve efficiency and reduce unit costs.

3. To grow profitably in an open, competitive environment.

4. To provide an environment where our people can achieve their potential and enhance our competitive advantage.

InterCity Values:

To deliver the strategy:

1. We will value our people, using their creativity to innovate and bring about continual improvement.

2. We will empower individuals and teams with responsibility and accountability.

3. We will behave with clarity, trust and openness, encouraging participation and giving support when needed.

BEHAVIOURS (for InterCity Staff)

Visibility
- Wear your InterCity name badge regularly
- Be accessible to our customers, staff and colleagues
- Take an interest in our staff and their work
- Take an interest in all aspects of service delivery to customers

Courtesy
- Greet members of staff: "Good Morning…etc"
- Introduce yourself to those you do not know
- Say "Thank You"
- Welcome visitors to meetings as guests
- Be gracious in all that you say, do and write

Personal Discipline
- Ensure you and others act in a safe way
- Be punctual for all meetings and engagements
- Value other people's time: as well as your own
- Honour your promises: do not make promises you cannot fulfil
- Own the problem and look for the solution
- Concentrate on one thing at a time
- Stick to the agenda
- Be appropriately dressed and groomed

Teamwork
- Share information: always ask "Who else should be told?"
- Practice collective responsibility for group decisions
- Establish protocols
- Know your teams' talents and use them
- No "Kitchen cabinets"

Respect
- Respect individuals and colleagues
- Respect other work groups, departments and businesses
- Respect our customers and suppliers
- Be positive: look for two good things in every contribution
- Confront: do not denigrate

Empathy
- Listen to and understand the position of others
- Be sensitive to other peoples' needs and feelings
- Encourage and support your colleagues
- Give feedback to colleagues
- Welcome and use feedback from colleagues

Enjoyment
- Have fun
- Celebrate successes
- Be passionate about our business

A DECADE BY DECADE HISTORY OF INTERCITY

1960s

1960s The Birth

● InterCity was born as a marketing concept in April 1966 when the name was used to brand services on the newly electrified West Coast route between Euston, Crewe and Manchester/Liverpool.

● By the end of 1966, InterCity had caught the public imagination and the name had spread to include the rest of British Rail's express passenger services and was later to be adopted by many European and World rail networks to designate their fast, quality services.

1970s Product Development

● By the early 1970s, with West Coast electrification completed to Glasgow (in 1974) and further electrification ruled out, it was becoming increasingly urgent to improve InterCity trains on conventional routes. The answer was found in the High Speed Train (HST) or InterCity 125, a world-beater from the beginning, which became for many the characteristic image of InterCity.

● With a maximum speed of 125 mph, HSTs were (and are still) the fastest diesel trains operating regularly on any railway in the world. Their Mark III coaches set a standard for InterCity with air-conditioning, double-glazing and wall-to-wall carpeting throughout and on every train was a restaurant or buffet car.

● The first route to benefit was Paddington to Bristol and South Wales where a full InterCity 125 service began in October 1976. Within the next few years the InterCity 125 network encompassed all the major non-electrified routes, enabling rail to meet the growing competition from motorways.

1970s

1980s

1980s Brand Development

● InterCity took on additional significance in 1982 when it was adopted as the 'company name' for a new business sector of British Rail which was set up to incorporate the long distance, high quality passenger services as a flagship brand. At first InterCity was a small planning and marketing organisation, but throughout the 1980s a closer identification of assets, took it onto an increasing business orientation.

● By the 1980s it was the turn of the East Coast route to benefit from major investment. In 1984, authorisation was given for electrification of the 400-mile route between London and Edinburgh and to build a new fleet of 31 InterCity 225 electric trains capable of 140 mph. Described as Britain's longest construction site, the £515m project involved altering almost 150 bridges to give clearance for the overhead wires. Later extended to Carstairs to enable electric working between Edinburgh and Glasgow, the project was completed on time and to budget, with train services inaugurated by The Queen in June 1991.

● In 1988/89 InterCity achieved profitability, becoming the first long distance passenger rail network in the world to operate with a surplus and without subsidy. Despite recession InterCity has maintained profitability over the ensuing five years.

1990s Profitable Business

● By the 1990s it was again the turn for investment of InterCity's West Coast route where much of the infrastructure, by now approaching 30 years old, was due for renewal. The £800m InterCity 250 project was developed, comprising a new fleet of InterCity 250 electric trains capable of 160 mph together with track improvement, upgrading of power supplies and modern signalling. With the recession, however, the InterCity 250 train has been shelved, though planned investment in infrastructure is to continue.

● In April 1992, after two years of railway reorganisation, InterCity became a fully fledged business within the British Rail umbrella, owning its track, stations and trains and employing the staff to operate and maintain them together with a separately identified customer service organisation.

● April 1994 saw the break up of InterCity into six train companies and numerous infrastructure companies. The InterCity brand name was retained.

1990s

INTERCITY – A CHRONOLOGY

1950
October
Daily Paddington-Wolverhampton, later Chester, train named 'The Inter-City' – first use of the term Inter-City.

1957
January
Diesel Multiple Units for Edinburgh-Glasgow route described as 'First inter-city express diesel trains'.

British Transport Commission Annual Report calls for three categories of express train – Pullman de luxe, special inter-city and ordinary express.

1960
July
Blue Pullmans introduced on London Midland Region and on Western Region in September.

1962
May
100 mph Deltic locomotives introduced on East Coast route.

1963
April
Term inter-city used in Beeching Report to describe general long distance express services.

1964
June
XP 64 project for carriage design introduced, many features became standard for later InterCity vehicles.

1965
January
British Railways Corporate Identity scheme introduced, bringing 'trade-name' of British Rail and double arrow logo.

1966
April 18th
Euston-Manchester and Liverpool electrification inaugurated.

InterCity created as marketing brand for new service.
New concepts in advertising introduced, using TV, press and mail shots.

Motorail first used as national marketing brand for Regional initiatives in accompanied car-carrying services.

December 5th
InterCity electric working via Birmingham commenced.

1967
March 6th
Reading-Heathrow Airport coach service introduced.

March
Major TV advertising campaign launched 'Inter-City: Heart to Heart'.

Business and Leisure Travel Service started at Birmingham New Street – one of the first Travel Centres.

1968

Transport Act – wiped out previous deficit amounting to £153m. Separation of commercial from social railways. Latter would be financially supported as long as Government thought necessary, former must work towards profitability.

September 23rd

Three month trial of automatic public address announcements on Euston-Manchester service.

London Midland Region introduce Line Group Management (eg West Coast/Midland/North East-South West etc) – precursors of InterCity management principles.

1969
April

InterCity Sleepers branding introduced.

June 30th

Rail Drive introduced – Car Hire at 70 InterCity stations in conjunction with Godfrey Davis, later with Hertz.

September

BR announce all new InterCity coaches will have air-conditioning.

North East-South West route to have InterCity status.

1970

InterCity fares raised (one of first examples of selective pricing).

February 23rd

Government approves Crewe-Glasgow electrification.

September 22nd

First Travel Centre opened on Western Region at Reading in Western Tower office building.

1971
January

British Railways Board first Corporate Plan published – InterCity required to bring in a 25% increase in revenue.

May 3rd

Paignton-Edinburgh service commenced.

May

Half-hourly InterCity service introduced between Edinburgh and Glasgow – first example of individual coaches in train sets branded 'Inter-City'.

May

Air conditioned Mark IId coaches introduced.

June

Travel Centres opened at Plymouth (10th) and Exeter (22nd).

Experimental Travel Centre at Reading moved to larger premises.

September

Success succeeds – German Railways introduce their express train network – also called InterCity.

1972
January

'Travelling' quarterly magazine for InterCity and other BR passengers published.

May 1st

Bristol Parkway opened – first station custom built in Parkway concept – out of town and close to motorway interchanges.

New Pudsey was designated a Parkway in late 1960s, this was an existing station, with car parking increased to encourage people to use rail between Leeds/Bradford, sponsored by local Passenger Transport Executive.

May

Euston-Birmingham half-hourly service introduced, together with re-cast of North East/South West services makes Birmingham hub of InterCity network.

July 25th
First run of experimental gas turbine powered Advanced
Passenger Train.

1973
January
Prototype of 125mph High Speed Diesel Train
commenced trials.

May 7th
Alfreton & Mansfield Parkway opened – station reopened
as a Parkway with heavy Local Authority support.

June
Air-conditioned Mark IIe coaches introduced on the
Bristol and South Wales routes.

June
New style InterCity tickets introduced.

July 2nd
Executive Travel concept introduced on services from
Newcastle/Leeds/Bradford to London.

July 16th
New station opened at Stevenage, promoted as InterCity
(London) peripheral station.

1974
May 6th
Electric services between Crewe and Glasgow inaugurated.

May 6th
All Line timetable for whole BR system first introduced.

1975
May 5th
Prototype High Speed Train enters revenue service
Paddington-Bristol.

May 12th
Mark III coaches introduced on Euston-Liverpool route.

Mark III coaches first to have accommodation for
wheelchairs by easy removal of seat and table.

Kelloggs cereals – free tickets for children promotion
launched.

1976
January 26th
Birmingham International station opened.

April 1st
Senior Citizen Railcard introduced.

October 4th
Production High Speed Trains introduced on Paddington
to Bristol and South Wales routes, marketed as 'Inter-City
125', branding carried on all vehicles in train.

In ten years of InterCity concept, business up by 35%.

1977
September 7th
First InterCity 125 Trains for Kings Cross-Edinburgh
delivered.

Big City Saver fares introduced (London-Sheffield/
Edinburgh/Glasgow).

October
Full InterCity 125 service introduced on the Bristol and
South Wales routes.

InterCity passengers up by 6% in 1977.

1978
May 8th
Initial InterCity 125 trains into revenue earning service on
Kings Cross-Edinburgh route.

June 7th
Prototype electric Advanced Passenger Train (155mph)
introduced. New livery later adopted as InterCity standard.
In first two years of InterCity 125 operations on Bristol
and South Wales routes ten million passengers carried,
business up by 33%.

July
New styles of uniform introduced throughout British Rail.

1979
May 14th
Full 125 services scheduled to start on East Coast route to Edinburgh, but delayed until August, due to collapse of Penmanshiel Tunnel.

May 14th
Two 125 services (0800 and 0905 ex Kings Cross) are publicised as third fastest trains in the World after two Japanese Shinkansen trains.

June 17th
Family Railcard introduced.

New indicator at Newcastle specifically shows 'Inter City Arrivals'.

September
Lever Bros joint promotion – free tickets with soap coupons until June 1980.

October
Initial introduction of InterCity 125 trains on Paddington-Penzance route.

HST concept and technology sold to Australia.

1980
January
Norman Fowler (Minister of Transport) in lecture in USA states that InterCity, Freight and Parcels should be run commercially – 'Government sees no reason why taxpayer should support InterCity.'

May 12th
Full 125 service on Paddington to Penzance route.

May 12th
Bus service Kettering-Corby-Peterborough introduced, promoted as part of InterCity service, through tickets, connections etc.

May 19th
East Coast 125 trains increased from eight to nine coaches to alleviate overcrowding.

July 14th
Minister of Transport announces private capital to be introduced to BR non-rail subsidiaries.

October
Coach deregulation creates major competition for InterCity.

Boarding Pass regulations on Summer Saturday trains to West of England first issued.

Jimmy Savile first used in advertising.

Humphrey Todd at British Rail Headquarters referred to as Passenger Manager (Inter City).

1981
January 5th
InterCity 125 introduced on Humberside and Teeside routes.

July 27th
Smoking banned in refreshment vehicles on Western Region 125 services.

September
Computerised reservations system introduced for East Coast.

September
Rail tickets for grocery purchases promotion until April 1982.

First 125 services on Cross Country route (ex North East-South West)

Saver Fares introduced Liverpool-London.

InterCity Europe launched – a relaunch of BR International sector and not directly connected with Inter-City internal services.

December 7th
Advanced Passenger Train enters revenue earning service.

1982
January 4th
Sector Management introduced by British Railways Board.

InterCity adopted as 'Company name' for new independent Sector.

Cyril Bleasdale appointed first Sector Director, InterCity.

January
Saver Fares introduced nationally.

Mark III sleeping cars introduced on East Coast route.

May 14th
Milton Keynes opened as InterCity station – later transferred to Network SouthEast.

May 17th
Nightrider cheap overnight fares London to Scotland introduced.

May 17th
Full 125 services on Cross Country route.

September 7th
25 million miles covered by East Coast 125 trains since May 1978 – ceremony at Newcastle station.

October 4th
125 trains introduced on St Pancras-Sheffield route.

Space Invader video games in buffet of Clansman (Euston-Inverness).

Swiss Railways adopt Inter City as brand name for express services.

1983
January 20th
Serpell Report on Railway Finances published. Saw no prospect of InterCity viability by 1985 as projected.

June 9th
Conservatives re-elected and pledged to privatise all state-owned enterprises, including railways.

June 16th
Executive travel targeted in Executive Travel Packages.

July 11th
Mark III sleepers introduced on Paddington-Penzance route.

Five-year, £18 million refurbishment programme of 1300 InterCity coaches announced.

APT livery to become InterCity standard for October relaunch of InterCity.

October 1st
Selby Diversion opened, avoiding mining developments, reducing East Coast journey times.

1984
January 5th
On-train public telephones introduced on Paddington–Swansea trains.

May 14th
West Coast maximum speed increased from 100mph to 110mph.

May 14th
Sandwell & Dudley – new InterCity station opened.

May

New InterCity livery applied to Gatwick Express trains (still managed by Network SouthEast).

July 27th

£306 million East Coast electrification scheme authorised by Government.

October

British Railways Board Corporate Plan projects turning of estimated £107m loss into £5m profit for InterCity in five years. 'InterCity into Profit' Policy Statement on same theme published in December.

Travellers Fare launches new concepts in train catering – (modular catering etc).

December

Port Talbot designated Parkway upon modernisation.

December

Charter Train Unit to be incorporated as part of InterCity Sector.

1985

January

'We're Getting There' advertising campaign launched, mostly on TV.

January

ScotRail formed – Edinburgh-Glasgow route transferred to Provincial Sector.

March

Hyphen dropped in 'InterCity' by March. NB APT-P Prototype carried 'InterCity APT' logo from 1980.

March 22nd

First Pullman Lounge opened at Kings Cross.

April

InterCity Charter Train Unit launched.

April

InterCity takes over Gatwick Express, London-Norwich and London-Harwich Parkeston Quay boat trains.

May 13th

Electric services inaugurated between Liverpool Street and Ipswich.

May

Pullman concept relaunched on East and West Coasts.

May

Fares structure simplified.

June

First train toilet adapted for disabled travellers on Mark III on London-Glasgow route.

July 29th

Didcot designated Parkway.

October 26th

Jetlink – Greenline coach links from Stevenage and Luton to Heathrow Airport.

November

INTERCITY magazine distributed free on train to First Class customers.

By end of 1985 all InterCity routes covered by computerised reservations and 130 InterCity trains have on-board telephones.

1986

February

Dr John Prideaux takes over as Sector Director.

March 6th

InterCity takes over on-train catering from Travellers Fare, InterCity On Board Services formed.

May 12th

Through services Brighton/Dover-Manchester/ Liverpool etc introduced, Kensington Olympia becomes InterCity station with Parkway characteristics – near M4 and M40, large car park etc.

May 12th

Lancashire Pullman introduced on the Blackpool to Euston route.

May 12th
Tiverton Parkway opened near M5 and North Devon Link Road.

May 12th
Telford Central station opened.

1987
May 1st
InterCity 21st Birthday celebrations commence with rebranding – new typeface for logo with swallow motif.

May 6th
InterCity Sleepers relaunch – introduction of Sleeper Lounge Reception Cars, Sleeper Check-in lounge opened at Euston.

May 11th
Second Class redesignated Standard.

May 11th
Electric services introduced between Liverpool Street and Norwich.

May
All principal services on Cross Country route InterCity125 operated.

May
'Master Cutler' Sheffield-St Pancras, 'Birmingham Pullman' Birmingham-Euston and 'Golden Hind' Plymouth-Paddington introduced.

June
Cuisine 2000 launched by InterCity Catering; shorebased food preparation and better menus etc.

October
APEX fares introduced London to West of Scotland.

November 18th
APTIS ticket issuing launched by Minister of Transport David Mitchell.

December
All rolling stock allocated to Sectors – InterCity now owns its own trains.

December 2nd
Advanced Passenger Train project abandoned.

1988
February 1st
Silver Standard introduced for Standard Class customers.

May
Euston becomes London terminus for all Scottish Sleeper services.

October 3rd
Through InterCity trains from Bradford to London commence.

October 3rd
Train Crew Agreements paves the way for introduction of Senior Conductor grade on InterCity trains.

October
Willesden Brent Depot renamed Willesden InterCity Depot.

December 14th
Push/pull working introduced on the West Coast (Wolverhampton-Euston service), using converted InterCity 125 power cars adapted to Driving trailers.

All InterCity trains now have on-board telephones.

1989
Financial year 1988/89 InterCity achieves profitability, one year earlier than projected. First main line railway in world to do so. InterCity no longer eligible for support payments from Government.

April 4th
New passenger complex opened at Reading. New InterCity concept of ticket sales and information services combined, also with shopping facilities etc.

May
Senior Conductors introduced, new style uniform, high profile image.

May 15th
Electric trains commenced working on Kings Cross-Leeds services.

September 20th
Inaugural run of InterCity 225 (Class 91 locomotive and Mark IV coaches) on Kings Cross-Leeds service, public services commenced October 2nd.

1990
February 27th
Frequent Traveller scheme launched, giving incentives and rewards package for regular InterCity travellers. Scheme withdrawn in 1991 due to lack of support.

February
Contracts awarded to supply Automatic Train Protection equipment to Great Western as one of two experimental installations on BR, to be operative in 1991.

May 14th
Special InterCity commuter trains introduced Kings Cross-Peterborough and St Pancras-Derby, with refurbished high density Mark IIf coaches.

June
£800 million upgrade of West Coast announced (cancelled in July 1992 due to financial situation).

October 1st
Push/pull operations commence on Anglia route.

1991
March
Refurbishment of Gatwick Express fleet commenced.

March 18th
Electrification of Carstairs-Edinburgh line inaugurated. Sponsored by InterCity Cross Country.

June 12th
First through public electric service London to Edinburgh, inaugurated by HM The Queen.

July 8th
InterCity 125 trains introduced on Poole to North services.

July
Glasgow-Edinburgh service (re)-introduced by InterCity complementing Regional Railways service.

September 26th
Record breaking InterCity 225 run Kings Cross-Edinburgh.

September 30th
InterCity 125 trains commence on Euston-Holyhead service.

September
First Boots promotion – September 1991-March 1992 (13 million vouchers issued worth four million journeys and £16 million revenue).

1992
January 6th
Chris Green appointed as Managing Director.

January
Free reservations for First Class and free tea/coffee for Pullman customers.

March 4th
Passenger's Charter announced.

April 6th
Under BRB Organising for Quality programme, InterCity established as a fully independent business, owning its own infrastructure, staff, trains etc. Chris Green designated Managing Director.

May
Super Apex Fares introduced London-Scotland.

May 11th
Stagecoach, a Scottish-based bus and coach company, take over marketing and sales of seats on overnight train Aberdeen-Euston, six Mark IId coaches leased to Stagecoach, they issue own tickets and staff trains.

June
Richard Branson discusses with Chris Green possibilities of Virgin running trains in partnership with InterCity.

July
Richard Branson in discussion with Transport Secretary – possibility of Virgin taking over a number of InterCity routes.

July
Government publishes White Paper on their plans for privatisation of the Railways.

First Customer Welcome team starts at Bristol Temple Meads; concept soon extended to 40 stations.

September 16th
Major InterCity marketing and service improvements package launched to combat recession – pronounced success within two months.

October
Boots offer repeated until March 1993.

November 1st
Stagecoach withdraw from lease and participation arrangements. Coaches returned to InterCity, BR tickets now valid on seated overnight trains, Stagecoach tickets still also valid.

December 9th
All Party Parliamentary Group of MPs formed to lobby for investment for West Coast.

Sleeper and Motorail combined into a separate InterCity management team – Overnight Services.

1993
January
Passenger's Charter becomes operative.

February 3rd
Railways Bill receives second reading, privatisation to go ahead. First franchises to include East Coast, Great Western and Gatwick Express.

March 29th
Spring campaign launched to build on marketing success of September 1992 campaign.

April
Government announces £150m available for leasing of one fleet of new trains – InterCity makes case for InterCity 225 for West Coast, competing against Network SouthEast who want new Networker trains.

May
InterCity Shuttle concept launched on West Midlands, Midland and Anglia routes.

June
Government announces remaining passenger franchises – of InterCity-West Coast/Midland/Anglia/Cross Country.

October 4th
Great Western Paddington to Bristol and South Wales also designated InterCity Shuttle.

October 10th

Gatwick Express established as first full shadow franchise. Fully independent operation, owning and having responsibility for staff and trains, contracting lease of stations and track capacity. No longer marketed as an InterCity route.

October 13th

British Railways Board announces that £150m rolling stock lease goes to NSE for 40 x Network Express trains. InterCity withdraw from competition as lease terms for 12 x IC225 considered too expensive from GEC-Alsthom.

October 28th

InterCity first Gateway station launched – Luton. Gateway concept – ample secure car parking – more frequent train service, avoiding London (Interchange with Network SouthEast). Customer Welcome teams. Other Gateways to be Reading-Stevenage-Watford Junction.

October 31st

Stagecoach joint marketing arrangement cancelled completely. British Rail continues to provide seats on Aberdeen-London service.

November 8th

InterCity telesales office opened in Newcastle. Freephone number nationally available, information by phone, tickets by return of post. Later by electronic mail to local station. Most modern of its kind in Europe.

November 30th

Budget speech – Chancellor Kenneth Clarke – announces £600 million to be found from private sector to upgrade infrastructure south of Crewe on West Coast.

1994

January 3rd

InterCity's last corporate television advertisement launched: 'Get Motoring' from Saatchi & Saatchi.

January 13th

First HST with central door locking introduced on Great Western as start of £17m investment programme for InterCity fleet.

February 4th

InterCity authorised first self-help credit card machines for pilot introduction at Euston.

February 9th

First of the Tribute ticket issuing machines launched at St Pancras Travel Centre and Newcastle Telesales, beginning of £17m introduction at all InterCity and European Passenger Services ticket offices.

March 1st

Completion of Platform Zoning at all InterCity stations.

March 26th

InterCity's final locomotive naming ceremony at Paddington. HST Power Car 'InterCity'.

March 31st

Closure of InterCity as a corporate business with a final profit of £100m.

April 1st

'Privatisation' organisation starts with a new Railtrack company and InterCity broken into six train operating companies.

May 29th

New 1994 Connecting Timetable introduced following close co-operation between the old InterCity, Regional Railways and Network SouthEast.

InterCity – Its People

InterCity Staff
At its peak in mid-1993, InterCity employed over 30,000 staff

Infrastructure Engineering — *12,144*

Station Retail — *4,986*

Fleet Engineering — *3,913*

Operations — *2,627*

On-Board Services — *2,085*

Drivers — *1,816*

Senior Conductors — *1,024*

Route Headquarters — *1,023*

InterCity Headquarters — *655*

Total Staff = 30,273

From 1992 InterCity's workforce was led by Managing Director Chris Green who is seen here with his fellow directors from the headquarters functions and the operating routes.

INTERCITY – ITS CUSTOMERS

The Passenger's Charter illustrated InterCity's commitment to improving customer service. It brought clear, numerate statements on basic customer performance targets and a new compensation scheme enabling a consistent and positive response to be given when things went wrong.

As part of the Passenger's Charter, InterCity displayed at major stations monthly and annual moving average tables of timekeeping and service reliability. InterCity also undertook to publish customer satisfaction research covering needs beyond basic reliability and these results reflected an encouraging level of customer satisfaction.

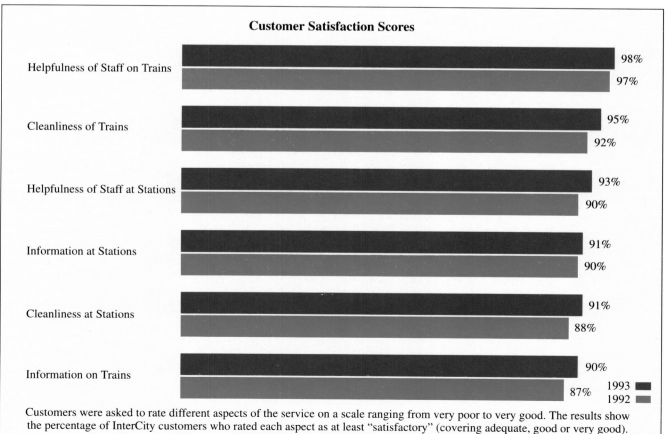

Customer Satisfaction Scores

	1993	1992
Helpfulness of Staff on Trains	98%	97%
Cleanliness of Trains	95%	92%
Helpfulness of Staff at Stations	93%	90%
Information at Stations	91%	90%
Cleanliness at Stations	91%	88%
Information on Trains	90%	87%

Customers were asked to rate different aspects of the service on a scale ranging from very poor to very good. The results show the percentage of InterCity customers who rated each aspect as at least "satisfactory" (covering adequate, good or very good).

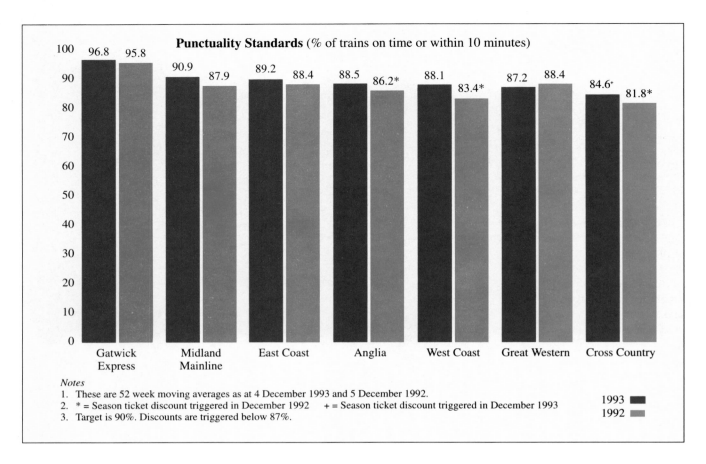

Punctuality Standards (% of trains on time or within 10 minutes)

Gatwick Express: 96.8 (1993), 95.8 (1992)
Midland Mainline: 90.9 (1993), 87.9 (1992)
East Coast: 89.2 (1993), 88.4 (1992)
Anglia: 88.5 (1993), 86.2* (1992)
West Coast: 88.1 (1993), 83.4* (1992)
Great Western: 87.2 (1993), 88.4 (1992)
Cross Country: 84.6+ (1993), 81.8* (1992)

Notes
1. These are 52 week moving averages as at 4 December 1993 and 5 December 1992.
2. * = Season ticket discount triggered in December 1992   + = Season ticket discount triggered in December 1993
3. Target is 90%. Discounts are triggered below 87%.

1993 ■
1992 ■

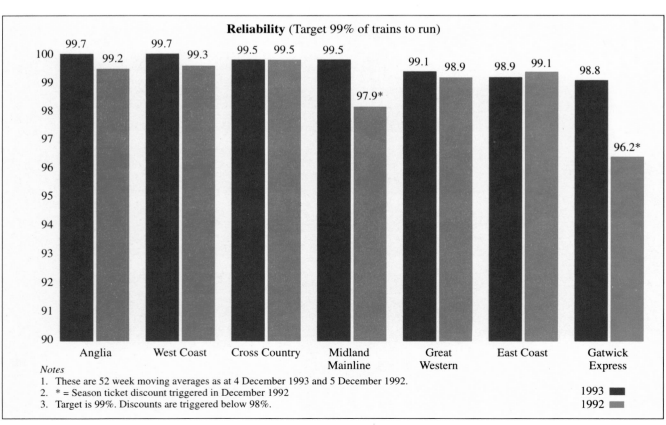

Reliability (Target 99% of trains to run)

Anglia: 99.7 (1993), 99.2 (1992)
West Coast: 99.7 (1993), 99.3 (1992)
Cross Country: 99.5 (1993), 99.5 (1992)
Midland Mainline: 99.5 (1993), 97.9* (1992)
Great Western: 99.1 (1993), 98.9 (1992)
East Coast: 98.9 (1993), 99.1 (1992)
Gatwick Express: 98.8 (1993), 96.2* (1992)

Notes
1. These are 52 week moving averages as at 4 December 1993 and 5 December 1992.
2. * = Season ticket discount triggered in December 1992
3. Target is 99%. Discounts are triggered below 98%.

1993 ■
1992 ■

INTERCITY – FINANCE & INVESTMENT

		1982	1983	1984/85†	1985/86	1986/87	1987/88	1988/89	1989/90	1990/91	1991/92	1992/93
Income/Turnover	£m	350	439	685	613	658	733	803	833	892	897	889
Operating (loss) (as published)	£m	(196)	(159)	(172)	(117)	(99)	(86)	–	–	–	–	–
Operating profit (at 1993/94 conventions)	£m		–	–	–	–	–	153	149	132	102	82
Receipts per train mile	£	na	na	14.65	16.18	17.16	18.19	18.69	18.69	18.33	17.69* [17.27]	17.54
Receipts per passenger mile	pence	na	na	9.82	10.36	10.71	10.73	11.17	11.63	11.68	11.37* [11.10]	11.20
Passenger miles per loaded train mile	passengers	na	na	155	161	165	175	174	167	162	160	161
Total operating expenses per train mile	£	na	na	20.93	19.88	20.20	19.70	17.42	18.68	18.01	15.64* [17.64]	16.00

* restated 1991/92, originally reported figures in [square] brackets
† 15 month period (change from calendar to fiscal year accounting)

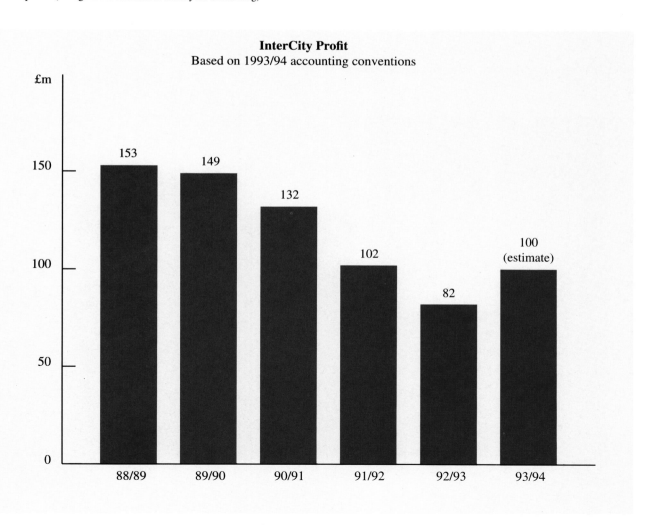

InterCity Profit
Based on 1993/94 accounting conventions

InterCity Investment

Recent reductions in funding and the ongoing recession have led to a significant decrease in the money available for investment. As most of InterCity's assets have a 30 year life cycle, this decline has created a backlog of modernisation and replacement work for future years and has slowed down the process of customer service improvement.

InterCity's 1993/4 Investment Plan

	£m
Track Renewals	41.0
Signalling and Track Projects	5.8
Electrification Projects	0.1
Telecommunications	0.9
Engineering Equipment	1.1
Road Vehicles	1.5
Traction and Rolling Stock	4.9
Terminals and Facilities	11.2
Stabling and Servicing Facilities	1.0
Computer and Other Projects	2.5
Total	70.0

InterCity Investment (total, including track renewals)

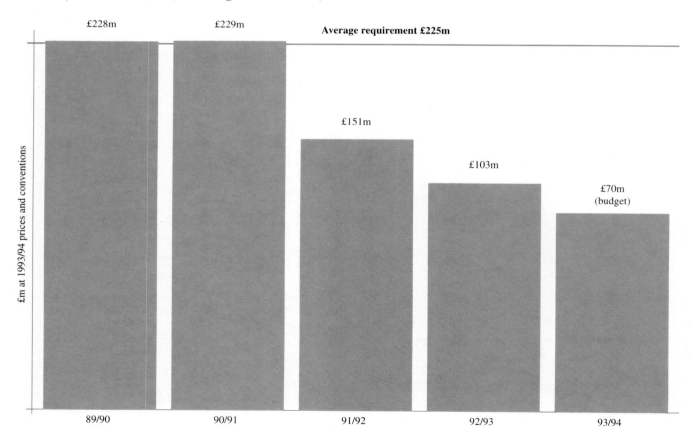

£228m   £229m   Average requirement £225m

£151m

£103m

£70m (budget)

£m at 1993/94 prices and conventions

89/90   90/91   91/92   92/93   93/94

172

INTERCITY – MARKETING

InterCity's comprehensive range of products enabled customers to travel by train and to enjoy a variety of services, tailored to meet their expectations and pocket.

InterCity For Business
First Class Pullman

First Class Pullman offered a choice of light refreshments or full breakfast, lunch and dinner. Personal service of hot and cold snacks and drinks served at seat, allowed uninterrupted working or the opportunity to just sit back and relax. First Class Pullman customers received complimentary tea and coffee, as well as all the benefits associated with First Class travel.

First Class

First Class accommodation was spacious and luxurious, and provided the ideal environment for the business traveller. All First Class tickets allowed access to the First Class Pullman Lounges at Euston, Kings Cross, Leeds, Newcastle and Edinburgh.

Silver Standard

Silver Standard was designed for the cost conscious business traveller, offering enhanced levels of comfort and service for those travelling on full fare Standard tickets. It was available on selected InterCity trains, on routes and at times which were most used by business people. Silver Standard included an at seat service of hot meals and refreshments, complimentary tea or coffee and snacks.

InterCity For Leisure
Leisure Tickets

InterCity offered a range of leisure tickets to suit every customer. Savers and SuperSavers offered flexibility, while advance purchase tickets including SuperApex and Apex gave excellent value for money to customers who were able to plan their journeys in detail before they travelled. Fare levels were competitive with coach and air travel, indeed Apex fares offered the lowest cost per mile in real terms since nationalisation of the railways in 1948.

Weekend First

At weekends and Bank Holidays, holders of many Standard tickets could travel in First Class for a small supplement. This made better use of First Class accommodation at these times, generated extra revenue for InterCity, and offered an uncomplicated First Class deal for many weekend travellers.

Leisure First

For customers who intended spending a Saturday night away, Leisure First offered First Class comfort at half the First Class Return fare for journeys to and from London. Leisure First had to be booked in advance and included free seat reservations.

Voyager

A competitively priced travel package, Voyager was designed to set new standards in comfort and style for the long-distance traveller. Initially it was available on selected trains between Scotland and the West Country, and featured guaranteed seats in Voyager accommodation, dedicated host/ess service, complimentary meals, or tea and coffee, all served to the customer at their seat.

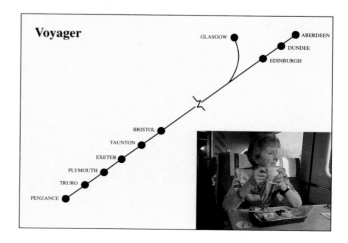

Voyager

GLASGOW • — • ABERDEEN
• DUNDEE
• EDINBURGH

BRISTOL •
TAUNTON •
EXETER •
PLYMOUTH •
TRURO •
PENZANCE •

InterCity Shuttle

With a high level of customer service, InterCity Shuttle was introduced on a number of key routes to and from London to win market share from the car. InterCity Shuttle was introduced between Euston and the West Midlands, St. Pancras and the East Midlands, Liverpool Street and East Anglia, and from Paddington to Bath, Bristol and South Wales.

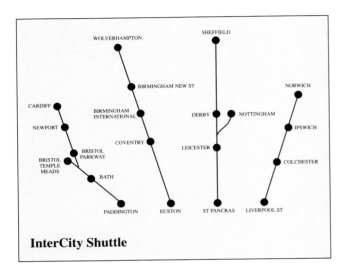

InterCity Shuttle

InterCity Sleepers

InterCity Sleepers offered a choice of First Class single cabins or Standard twin-berth cabins. All were air-conditioned with private washing facilities. An attentive steward/ess welcomes the traveller aboard. In First Class, a complimentary light breakfast and morning newspaper was provided (except on Sunday mornings) while in Standard the traveller was offered early morning tea or coffee and biscuits.

On each train the Lounge Car offered a relaxing club atmosphere in which to unwind with a drink or snack before retiring. For those requiring a more substantial start to the day, breakfast was served in the Lounge Car.

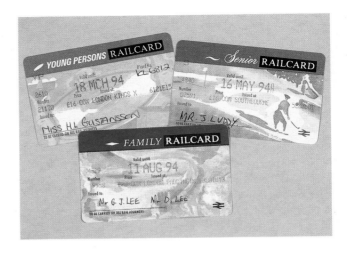

Railcards

InterCity managed BR's range of Railcards – for Seniors, Young People and Students, and for Families – which gave discounts on most types of tickets. In 1992/3 InterCity gained £140m (17%) of its revenue from Railcards, representing 13m (21% of) InterCity journeys.

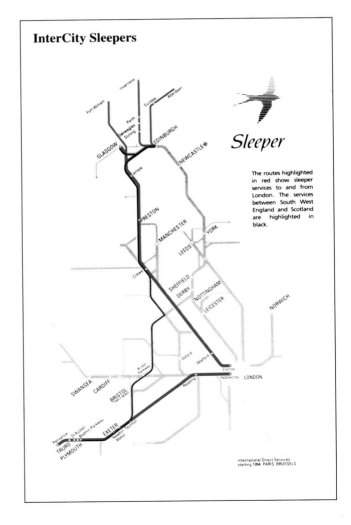

InterCity Sleepers

Sleeper

The routes highlighted in red show sleeper services to and from London. The services between South West England and Scotland are highlighted in black.

International Direct Services starting 1994 PARIS BRUSSELS

InterCity Motorail

Motorail combined the comfort of InterCity travel with the convenience of having one's own car at the destination. It was the civilised alternative to motorway driving.

Cars travelled in secure covered vans on the same train while the customer relaxed in First Class air-conditioned comfort by daytime service or with the choice of single or twin berth Sleeper cabins on overnight services.

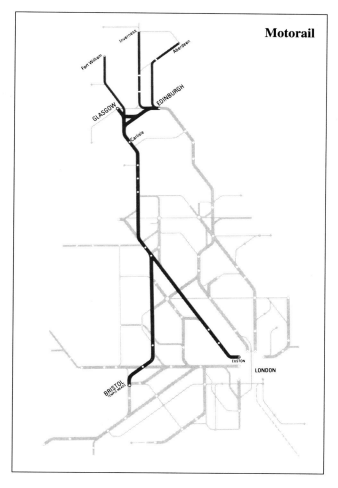

Motorail

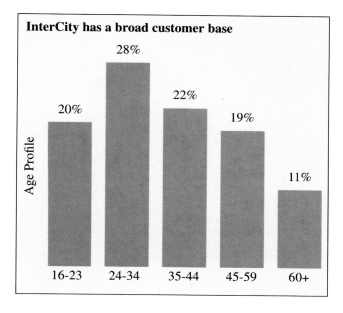

InterCity has a broad customer base

Age Profile

- 16-23: 20%
- 24-34: 28%
- 35-44: 22%
- 45-59: 19%
- 60+: 11%

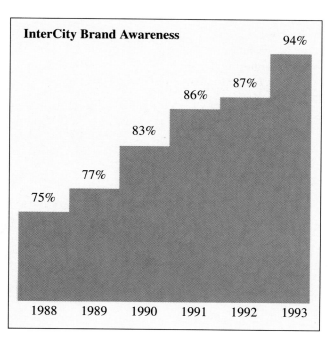

InterCity Brand Awareness

- 1988: 75%
- 1989: 77%
- 1990: 83%
- 1991: 86%
- 1992: 87%
- 1993: 94%

Boots Promotion 1991-93

Shell Promotion 1993-94

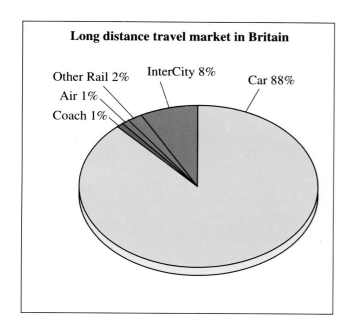

Long distance travel market in Britain

Other Rail 2%
Air 1%
Coach 1%
InterCity 8%
Car 88%

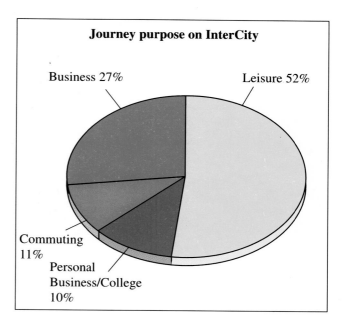

Journey purpose on InterCity

Business 27%
Leisure 52%
Commuting 11%
Personal Business/College 10%

	1987/88	1988/89	1989/90	1990/91	1991/92	1992/93
Passenger Journeys (million)	75	72	71	70	66	62
Passenger Miles (million)	8200	8300	8100	7900	7800	7600
Average Journey Length (miles)	109	115	114	113	118	122
Customers per day (000's)	207	198	195	191	182	171
Trains per day	–	–	–	–	780 *	775 *

* Includes Gatwick Express

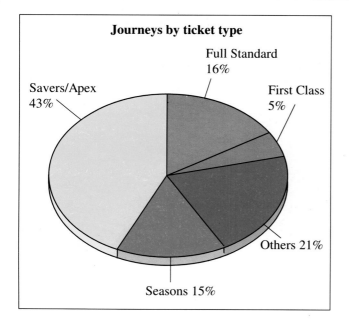

Journeys by ticket type

Full Standard 16%
Savers/Apex 43%
First Class 5%
Others 21%
Seasons 15%

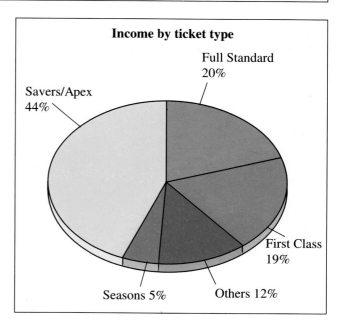

Income by ticket type

Full Standard 20%
Savers/Apex 44%
First Class 19%
Others 12%
Seasons 5%

Derby

Euston

INTERCITY – A NATIONAL NETWORK

Through trains Mondays to Fridays in 1993

	Distance (miles)	Number of trains	Fastest journey (hr:min)	Average speed (mph)
London to:				
Reading	36	60	:22	98
Swindon	77	45	:50	93
Bristol Parkway	112	22	1:15	89
Bristol Temple Meads	118	23	1:29	79
Cardiff Central	145	21	1:52	78
Exeter St. Davids	174	15	2:02	85
Norwich	115	19	1:34	73
Peterborough	76	36	:46	99
Doncaster	156	31	1:33	101
Leeds	186	19	2:05	89
Newcastle-upon-Tyne	269	26	2:39	101
Edinburgh	393	15	4:06	96
Glasgow Central	401	13	4:59	81
Birmingham New Street	113	33	1:35	72
Manchester Piccadilly	184	17	2:31	73
Liverpool Lime Street	193	15	2:33	76
Preston	209	15	2:22	88
Leicester	99	32	1:08	88
Derby	128	18	1:34	82
Nottingham	126	16	1:37	78
Sheffield	165	15	2:11	76
Cross Country **Birmingham New Street to:**				
Bristol Temple Meads	89	16	1:20	67
Plymouth	217	10	3:20	65
Bournemouth	175	8	3:28	50
Glasgow Central	297	4	4:20	69
Edinburgh	295	7	4:24	67
Newcastle-upon-Tyne	210	8	3:17	64
Manchester Piccadilly	82	14	1:34	52
Brighton	186	2	3:45	50

Bridge renewal in progress

One of the latest signalling control centres

INTERCITY – ROUTE BY ROUTE

	Anglia	East Coast	Great Western	Midland	West Coast	Cross Country	InterCity Total
System							
Route Miles	125†	493	467	161	531	213	1865
% Electrified	100†	100	0	33	94	2	58
Track Miles	250†	1309	1557	548	1446	476	5336
% Electrified	100†	97	0	40	93	3	53
Trains operated Mon-Fri	47	104	135	68	174	102	630
Infrastructure							
Bridges/Culverts	†	2353	1748	1500	3373	1300	10274
Tunnels	†	42	33	28	31	14	148
Signalboxes	†	9	20	5	45	13	92
Points/Switches	†	1193	1860	985	2148	1263	7449
Signals	†	3292	3479	890	3580	873	12114
Stations	3	13	21	8	22	1	68
Carriage Washing Machines	1	2	12	2	6	1	24

† Owned by Network SouthEast

INTERCITY: HIGH SPEED RUNS

Spoiled for choice for particular logs of train running, it was decided to demonstrate some of the variety available by selecting one recording taken of the first run in revenue service of the APT in 1981 and one taken from the inauguration of the Anglia Electrics from London to Norwich in 1987. Information for both was provided by Peter Semmens who has often acted as official timekeeper on special, high-speed trains.

The Inaugural APT Run 1981

The first service run of the Advanced Passenger Train reached London from Glasgow just over a minute early on 7th December 1981, having achieved a maximum speed of 138 mph and averaged 102.3 mph from Preston. The 208.9 miles from there to Euston were run in 122 minutes 34 seconds, seven minutes inside schedule, in spite of two 50 mph and two 20 mph permanent-way slacks.

The train consisted of a special formation, with one articulated six-car passenger-carrying set behind two power cars. At the front end there was a driving trailer and another articulated trailer brake for the test staff. We thus had 8,000 horsepower available for a tare weight of 360 tons, giving a power/weight ratio of 22 hp/ton. Where I was able to record the acceleration, it was remarkable. Recovering from one 20 mph permanent-way check, we reached 92 mph in two miles *up the concluding section of the climb to Shap!*

Starting from Glasgow at 07.00 on a December morning with the occasional snow flurry about in a new type of high-speed train is not calculated to give optimum conditions for recording speeds. Indeed it was not really until we were over the border at Gretna that it became light enough to see the mileposts. By Beattock, I had managed to acclimatise myself sufficiently to the rhythm of the articulated bogies to count rail joints, so was able to clock-up a maximum of 129 mph before Lockerbie. We were by this time running about 8½ minutes late. Although we had left Motherwell three-quarters of a minute early, we suffered a three-minute signal stop just after Carluke, caused by a track-circuit failure, so that by Carstairs we were well down on schedule. In spite of a four-minute recovery margin leaving the Scottish Region, we were still 4½ minutes late as we rolled through Carlisle at the regulation 20 mph.

The climb to Shap was most interesting. Before Wreay we were over the "ton" and had to slow from 114 to the APT restriction of 90 through Penrith. Then we reached 116 again before the second 90 slowing at the site of the former Eden Valley Junction. A brief acceleration preceded the relaying slack already mentioned, but on the descent of Shap we again clocked-up a full 125 going down the bank.

Thanks to the various checks we were eight minutes late at Tebay. There is no real chance to run continuously at high speed until after Oxenholme, but we then had a spell of some 15 miles at about the 125 mark. The APT is allowed 100 through Lancaster, but we were rather more modest although we then reached a maximum of 126 before Preston in the course of covering the 15 miles to Milepost 2 at an average of exactly 125 mph. With the aid of a second recovery margin we reached the last intermediate stop under four minutes late. Our two-minute station time was extended, however, and we finally left for London six minutes late.

Just before Preston I moved from the leading coach of the six-car rake to have breakfast in the dining car, and was immediately struck with the better riding of the latter vehicle. The tilt mechanism seemed exemplary, and on numerous occasions I looked up from something I was reading to find the horizon had completely changed its position without my being aware of the tilt coming on. There was a lot of vertical oscillation, however, and a number of sideways "biffs" which were well up to the Burlington Northern standard! I could not help recalling that on the first press run of the "Silver Jubilee," back in 1935, some very lively movements were reported, and even after the suspension was tightened up, the catering crew, so I understand, always used to remove the flower vases from the tables as the train left Kings Cross. For the record, my coffee stayed in the cup without spilling a drop for some twenty minutes during breakfast, with the level a quarter of an inch below the rim.

By Crewe, thanks to the next recovery margin, we were running only a minute late, and then came a fine acceleration up the bank to Whitmore. Whereas back in 1937 *Coronation* was driven flat out *down* the bank to achieve 112 mph, we accelerated up it to 126. Such is progress! Stafford gave us one of the best opportunities to see the whole train tilted over as we took the well-known curve at 85 mph, compared with the more usual limit of 60, and we were away for another 125 mph spell before the next relaying slack. At about this point someone clearly gave the crew the authority to start utilising more than the normal service speed of the train, and we had a rousing 131 before Rugby. Another was to follow after Kilsby Tunnel, but then at Blisworth we shot away to average 137 over 3¾ miles, with a maximum of 138.

Although there was, I believe, a "140 club" among some of the HST drivers in the early days before the speed cut-outs were fitted, our 138 is probably the fastest any fare-paying passengers have travelled in this country, and was checked by several independent recorders on the train.

After this we thought the punctual arrival at Euston was "in the bag," but there were two nasty late permanent-way checks, the second being to 20 at Wembley. Helped by the final recovery margin we were nevertheless able to roll in to the official welcome by Sir Peter Parker just over a minute early, a gratifying conclusion to the run.

Glasgow-Euston

Date: 7th December 1981
APT formation: 2 + 2 + 6
Power car Nos: SC 49002/3†
Load: empty/full (tons): 360/380

Dist		Sch	Actual		Speeds
Miles		mins	m	s	mph
0·0	GLASGOW CENTRAL	0	0	00	–
4·8	Cambuslang		7	47	83
6·4	Newton	8	8	54	90
8·3	Uddingston	9½	9	58	104
12·7	MOTHERWELL	13	12	57	–
7·5	Carluke		7	06	88
–			Sig stop		–
15·8	Carstairs	10½	18	23	107/92
39·7	*Summit*	22½	31	33	117
49·7	*Beattock*	27½	36	33	129
63·6	Lockerbie	34	43	10	128
–		[4]	–	–	–
80·8	*Gretna*	45	52	05	110
89·4	CARLISLE	53	58	14	20*
94·3	*Wreay*		62	52	107
107·3	Penrith	64½	69	33	114/90*
112·5	*Milepost 46*		72	34	116/90*
–			p.w.s.		93/20*
118·8	*Shap*		79	12	46
120·9	*Summit*		80	34	92
126·4	*Tebay*	74½	83	19	123
132·4	*Grayrigg*		86	50	87*/96
135·5	*Milepost 23*		88	35	112/92*
139·4	Oxenholme	83	90	54	114/124
152·3	Carnforth	89½	97	20	126
158·5	Lancaster	92½	100	28	87*
170·0	*Garstang*	[4]	106	55	126
179·5	PRESTON	109	113	23	–

Speed restrictions.

† Named "City of Derby."

Dist		Sch	Actual		Speeds
Miles		mins	m	s	mph
0·0	PRESTON	0	0	00	–
4·0	Leyland		3	58	111
10·5	*Milepost 11¼*		6	09	124
15·1	Wigan	9	9	37	128/90 *
20·0	*Golborne*		12	12	125/100 *
26·9	Warrington	16	16	16	120
34·5	*Weaver Junc.*	19½	19	45	126
43·5	Winsford	23	24	33	113
–		[4]	–	–	–
51·0	CREWE	34½	29	20	126/30 *
54·0	*Milepost 155*		32	23	102
59·0	*Milepost 150*		34	54	126
70·2	Norton Bridge	46	40	17	120
75·5	STAFFORD	48½	42	57	125/85 *
84·8	Rugeley		48	06	125
–			p.w.s.		20 *
92·8	Lichfield	57½	55	55	115
99·0	Tamworth	60½	58	54	123
111·9	Nuneaton	67	65	21	125/128
126·5	RUGBY	75	73	09	131/60 *
133·8	*Welton*		77	25	131
146·2	*Blisworth*		83	28	128/138
154·3	*Castlethorpe*	[4]	87	05	136
–			p.w.s.		50 *
162·4	BLETCHLEY	97	91	34	–
168·8	Leighton Buzzard		95	04	80 *
172·9	Cheddington		97	14	127
177·4	Tring	104	99	19	128
184·6	Hemel Hempstead		102	49	127
–			p.w.s.		50 *
191·6	WATFORD JUNC.	111	107	25	115 *
197·6	Harrow		110	19	127
–		[4]	p.w.s.		20 *
201·0	Wembley		113	04	–
204·0	*Milepost 5*	122½	115	42	103
208·9	EUSTON	129½	122	34	–

Speed restrictions.

The Inaugural Electric Run to Norwich in 1987

The Liverpool Street to Norwich electrification scheme was launched in spectacular fashion on May 5th 1987, when an inaugural special ran the 115.1 miles from Liverpool Street to Norwich in 83 minutes 22 seconds, in the course of which it achieved a flying average of exactly 100 mph over the 39 miles between Sproughton and Swainsthorpe.

These railway celebrations were combined with those for the 60th anniversary of the formation of the Round Table organisation, and the renamed locomotive, No. 86 220, *The Round Tabler*, looked splendid in its new InterCity livery, with its seven-coach train to match. The buffer stops on platform No. 8 are set well along from the original milepost zero, and I have assumed that our journey was four chains shorter as a result, while, at Norwich, with the locomotive virtually up to the buffer stops, the rear coach was eight chains further back.

Official time-keeper on the run was B. D. J. Walsh, President of the Great Eastern Railway Society, and he and I were both accommodated in the rear coach of the train, so the mileages quoted take account of the "lost" distances referred to above. With the exception of the time at Trowse, all the other information in the log is from Mr. Walsh, and I am most grateful to him for such a comprehensive set of figures, obtained under great difficulty, because of the high speeds and the smallness of the old GE mileposts, which were on the near side.

Although the exit from Liverpool Street in the Norwich direction is less restrictive than it is on the Cambridge line, it still took us the 15 miles to Harold Wood to achieve even time. We had touched 53 before the 50 mph slowing through Stratford, and Driver Arthur Edwards eased back from 71 at Forest Gate to 67 through Manor Park. By Goodmayes we were topping the 90-mark, and accelerated to no less than 91 before Harold Wood. The two miles at 1 in 108 were rushed at a minimum of 83 before the first of three slowings. These were to 47 just beyond the summit, and then came a more severe one to 20 through Ingatestone, but, such is the power of a class "86," that we touched 82 in between. Finally, having recorded a maximum of 93 before Chelmsford, we slowed to 51 beyond the station.

Clear of all this, we then set about some more sustained high-speed running, with two maxima of 104 before Marks Tey. Colchester was passed at a mere 88, and the slowing to 79 after Ardleigh was again preceded by a couple of 100-plus maxima, this time, though, of only 101. Beyond Manningtree we notched up 102 at Milepost 65, having marginally accelerated up the bank from Bentley. Then came the usual long slowing for the junctions and tunnel outside Ipswich, but we were through there at a restrained 30 mph in 52 minutes 33 seconds, having averaged 78.4 mph from Liverpool Street. Running non-stop through Ipswich has never been very common, and for the last two years all the through trains have been stopping at this point to change from electric to diesel power or *vice versa*.

Now, with the catenary in place all the way to Norwich, Driver Edwards was able to continue in fine style. As already mentioned, our average speed, pass-to-pass, between Sproughton and Swainsthorpe was exactly 100, and this was achieved with no greater variations than 95 at Tivetshall and 105 at Burston. Riding was lively at these speeds, but could by no means be said to have been uncomfortable. After Swainsthorpe the brakes went on for the complicated entry to Norwich, with the steep descent from Trowse Upper Junction, and the sharp left-hand curve after the swing-bridge at Trowse itself. This has been completely renewed as part of the electrification scheme, with the speed restriction raised to 40, and we were the first passenger-carrying train to go over it at the new limit.

Looking out of the window of my coach at the rear of the train, I noted, as we crossed, that there were some flashes between the pantograph and overhead electrification equipment. These were where gaps in the latter had had to be provided to allow the bridge to swing for river traffic. From the riding point of view, it was a lot smoother going over the corresponding gaps in the rails at this speed than it is over the swing-bridges across the ends of the Caledonian Canal, in the north of Scotland, where the restrictions are even more severe than the one used to be at Trowse.

As already mentioned, our final time to Norwich was 83 minutes 22 seconds, which corresponded to an average of 82.8 mph. In spite of a lot of research I had been unable to find any comparable non-stop diesel runs over this route, but almost thirty years ago "Britannia" No. 70039, *Sir Christopher Wren*, covered the distance in 118 minutes 21 seconds with a Crusaders' Union special organised by Cecil J. Allen. With his Great Eastern background, he would certainly have found the electric run on May 5th extremely stimulating, cutting, as it did, 30 per cent off the time of the steam run.

Liverpool Street-Norwich

Date: 5th May 1987
Locomotive: Bo-Bo
No: 86 220
Name: The Round Tabler
Load: No./empty/full (tons): 7/244/255

Dist Miles		Actual m s	Speeds mph
0·0	LIVERPOOL STREET	0 00	–
1·1	Bethnal Green	2 33	38
2·8	Bow Junc.	4 38	53
3·9	STRATFORD	6 03	50*
4·4	Maryland	6 34	68
5·2	Forest Gate	7 13	71
6·2	Manor Park	8 05	67
7·3	Ilford	9 03	76/79
8·5	Seven Kings	9 59	81
9·2	Goodmayes	10 31	77
10·0	Chadwell Heath	11 04	81/80
12·3	Romford	12 51	78/82
13·5	Gidea Park	13 42	80
14·9	Harold Wood	14 48	91/88
18·2	Brentwood	17 00	83/66*
19·2	Milepost 19¼	17 49	66*
–		t.r.s.	47*
20·2	SHENFIELD	18 48	82
–		t.r.s.	20*
23·6	Ingatestone	21 36	–/93
29·7	CHELMSFORD	27 02	68*

Dist Miles		Actual m s	Speeds mph
–		t.r.s.	51 *
35·8	Hatfield Peverel	31 26	100
38·6	Witham	33 02	102
42·2	Kelvedon	35 12	100/97
46·6	Marks Tey	37 48	104/95
51·6	COLCHESTER	40 52	88*/101
56·0	Ardleigh	43 42	101/79 *
59·4	Manningtree	45 47	90*/101
63·1	Bentley	48 19	101
76·8	Halifax Junc.	51 22	30 *
68·7	IPSWICH	52 33	30*/68
69·4	East Suffolk Junc.	53 24	82
73·5	Claydon	56 02	104
77·0	Needham Market	58 08	101
80·6	Stowmarket	60 16	98
82·9	Haughley	61 41	102
86·5	Finningham	63 50	98/101
91·3	Mellis	66 43	101
95·0	Diss	68 50	103
97·5	Burston	70 20	105
100·5	Tivetshall	72 12	95
104·0	Forncett	74 19	98
106·6	Flordon	75 82	101
109·7	Swainsthorpe	77 38	103/48 *
112·8	Trowse Upper Junc.	79 56	– *
114·1	Trowse	81 00	– *
114·5	Swingbridge Junc.	82 00	40 *
115·1	NORWICH	83 22	–

Speed restrictions.

185

INTERCITY – THE FLEET

InterCity Locomotives

Electric	Built	88/89	89/90	90/91	91/92	92/93
Class 91	1988-90	10	13	31	31	31
Class 90	1988	15	15	15	15	15
Class 87	1973-74	32	35	35	35	35
Class 86/4	1965-66	10	4	–	–	–
Class 86/2	1965-66	38	48	52	52	52
Class 86/1	1965-66	3	3	3	3	3
Class 81, 83, 85	1959-63	10	7	4	–	–
Class 73	1965-67	12	12	12	12	13
Diesel						
Class 43 (HST)	1976-82	197	197	197	197	195
Class 47	1963-67	78	88	81	60	39
Class 37	1960-65	3	3	4	4	9
Class 31	1957-62	–	–	–	–	6
TOTAL LOCOMOTIVES		**408**	**425**	**434**	**409**	**398**
Average age of locomotives (years)		–	–	–	**16.9**	**17.8**

Coaches/Driving Trailers (including catering vehicles)

	Built	88/89	89/90	90/91	91/92	92/93
Mark I	1955-64	230	227	183	118	125
Mark II abc	1965-70	148	165	95	–	–
Mark II de	1971-73	470	472	482	319	261
Mark II f	1973-75	442	443	446	456	455
Mark III	1975-86	266	266	298	298	298
Mark IV	1989-92	–	57	211	273	282
HST Trailers	1976-86	712	712	712	712	712
Mark III Sleeper	1981-84	186	186	192	191	141
Mark I Motorail	1958-60	64	64	64	64	55
Driving Trailers (non passenger)						
Mark I	1959	10	10	10	10	10
Mark III	1989-90	–	30	52	52	52
Mark IV	1989-91	–	8	27	32	32
TOTAL COACHES		**2528**	**2640**	**2772**	**2523**	**2423**
Average age of coaches (years)		–	–	–	**15.2**	**15.4**

Class 91

Class 91 locomotives were the power for the East Coast main line InterCity 225 trains. The 31 locomotives were constructed between 1988 and 1990 for GEC-TPL at BREL Crewe and were a total change from previous structural and technical electric locomotive designs. They had one raked cab end, for normal running at high-speeds and one 'slab' front end for operation at up to 90 mph. Although designed for 140 mph running, signalling constraints meant that they were limited to 125 mph. Under normal conditions the Class 91s were coupled at the northern end of Kings Cross – Leeds/Edinburgh/Glasgow services, being controlled in the southbound direction from Mark IV Driving Van Trailers (DVTs), control signals being passed to the remote locomotive through the train by TDM equipment.

Class 90

Class 90 electric locomotives were introduced from 1988 to replace earlier classes of electric locomotives on the West Coast main line. They were a derivative of the Class 87/1 and indeed, originally were to be known as Class 87/2. Built by BREL Ltd at Crewe, they were fitted from new with Time Division Multiplex push-pull equipment. In 1993 15 locomotives of the 50 built were owned by InterCity, and were usually found coupled to the northern end of Euston-Wolverhampton/Liverpool/Manchester or Anglo-Scottish services. The bulk of the class were employed on freight or parcels duties.

Class 89

Built in 1986, one-off locomotive No. 89001 was built by BREL at Crewe on behalf of Brush Traction, to demonstrate state-of-the-art equipment, which could be made available to InterCity. The locomotive, which had a top speed of 125 mph, operated many test and demonstration trains over the West Coast main line, prior to being allocated to Bounds Green and used on East Coast duties during the transition from diesel to electric power. After its useful demonstration period the locomotive was sold to the preservation movement.

The Class 89 was a total change from previous AC locomotive technology, using six-wheel bogies, this was considered as a potential improvement over the previous four-wheel configuration in terms of adhesion and traction characteristics.

Class 87

This fleet of thirty six locomotives was built to supplement the Class 86s on West Coast services, following electrification of the route from Weaver Junction to Glasgow, opening on 6th May 1974. The locomotives were basically a 1970s refinement of the previous AC types. They were built by BREL Crewe with electrical equipment supplied by GEC. The fleet was built with bogie gearing for 110 mph running, and over the ensuing twenty years of operation received pantograph modifications to permit high-speed operation. When constructed, multiple-control equipment using the conventional wire to wire system was fitted. After the widespread introduction of Time Division Multiplex equipment this was fitted as standard and the orginal system removed. The 87s were the first class to be built solely with air brake equipment, and the first to be built without train reporting indicators on the ends.

Locomotive No. 87101, built in 1975, was designated Class 87/1 and fitted with state-of-the-art thyristor traction equipment, as a prototype for next generation electric traction. It weighed only 79 tonnes, some four tonnes lighter than the main class. The locomotive retained this equipment and in 1993 was allocated to Railfreight Distribution.

Class 86

The largest single fleet of AC electric locomotives was the Class 86, of which 100 were built by BR and English Electric in 1965-66, following operating experience with the pioneer fleets. The locomotives were built with dual vacuum and air brakes and were used on the Euston-Manchester/Liverpool/Wolverhampton routes. From the late 1970s when it was proposed to increase speeds on the West Coast to 110 mph, tests were carried out to see if this was practicable. With this in mind, and a past history of rough riding and technical problems, a modified bogie design was formulated. This included large bogie/body 'Flexicoil' springs and internally rubber-cushioned wheels. These modifications were carried out to the majority of the class.

When introduced the Class 86s were all allocated to Willesden depot, but with InterCity's takeover of the Liverpool Street-Norwich/Harwich Parkeston Quay route in 1985, a batch of Class 86 locomotives was transferred to Norwich. On that route they were initially operated in the conventional way, however, from October 1st 1990 InterCity introduced push-pull working, with remote driving facilities being provided by Driving Brake Standard Open (DBSO) coaches. The push-pull systems used the latest Time Division Multiplex (TDM) technology.

The development of TDM technology also enabled a fleet of Mark III Driving Van Trailers (DVTs) to be built

for the West Coast. From late 1988 these permitted Class 86 locomotives, as well as Class 87s and 90s, to be semi-permanently coupled to the northern end of formations, with a DVT providing cab controls at the London end.

In 1993 InterCity operated a fleet of fifty five Class 86 locomotives from Willesden, Longsight and Norwich depots.

An artist's impression of an electrically hauled express passenger train passing the new signal box at Wilmslow, Cheshire

London Midland Electrification

MANCHESTER · LIVERPOOL · BIRMINGHAM · LONDON

LONDON MIDLAND *Getting on with the job*

Work on the first stage of the mammoth task of electrifying the London Midland Main Line is now over, and electric trains are running between Manchester and Crewe.
The next stage between Liverpool and Crewe will be finished by the end of 1961.

Class 81-85

These five AC electric classes were all constructed under the Modernisation Plan, by different manufacturers for use at the start of electrification in the North West. All types followed the same design brief and were very similar. When built the locomotives were only fitted for vacuum brake operation. However as the air-braking system was developed and became standard they received major refurbishment including air brakes; they were only built with electric train heat equipment.

As electrification of the West Coast was completed in April 1966 these five pioneer classes extended their operating range. Following introduction of Class 86 locomotives they were seen less often on front line duties, and were gradually withdrawn over the next two decades. They were the first electric locomotives to collect alternating current at high voltage (25,000 volts) and the first production BR locomotives to be built for 100 mph running.

Class 73

These dual power (electric/diesel) locomotives are some of the most versatile on BR. Built originally for Southern Region use, their involvement in InterCity operations was very limited until the re-launch of the Victoria-Gatwick Airport 'Gatwick Express' in May 1984. For this service – created by Southern Region – a fleet of modified Mark IIf coaches was formed into fixed sets. Class 73s were coupled at the Gatwick end of formations to provide power, whilst a fleet of Gatwick Luggage Vans was rebuilt from surplus electric multiple units to provide additional power and driving controls at the London end. Soon after its introduction the route was taken over by InterCity who eventually obtained dedicated locomotives which were re-classified Class 73/2. The entire fleet is kept at Stewarts Lane Depot. Class 73/2 locomotives work the Gatwick

Express service, and provide power for the Venice - Simplon - Orient Express private Pullman train and other InterCity charter services.

Class 43 (HST)

The power cars of the InterCity 125 are categorised as Class 43. Two are used in each High Speed Train – one at either end of a set of seven, eight or nine passenger coaches.

Cruising at speeds up to 125 mph, they are still the world's fastest diesel trains and are an everyday sight from the Highlands of Scotland to the west of Cornwall.

Developed in the early 1970s, the trains were built by BR at Crewe (power cars) and Derby (coaches) and the production trains entered passenger service in 1976 between London, Bristol and South Wales. By the early 1980s, IC125s were also serving South Wales, the West Country, the East Coast route to Yorkshire, the North East and Scotland, cross-country routes and the East Midlands. The latest development in 1991 saw them running on the West Coast route to Holyhead.

Class 55

The fleet of 22 production Deltic locomotives was built by English Electric and introduced to replace steam locomotives on the East Coast route to Scotland. They were a derivative of the prototype Deltic built in 1955, and were the first 100 mph main line diesel locomotives in Great Britain. The locomotives each had two Napier Deltic engines which gave a combined output of 3,300 hp. The name 'Deltic' came from the three banks of six cylinders arranged in a shape resembling the Greek symbol Delta.

The class was instrumental in developing the East Coast route and, when introduced in 1961, made it possible to cover the Kings Cross-Edinburgh route in six hours. Over the years this was considerably reduced and when the class was finally ousted by IC125s, the Kings Cross-Edinburgh timing was down to around five hours.

Class 52

This class, which was more usually referred to as the Western class as all names were prefixed 'Western', consisted of 74 2,700 hp diesel-hydraulic locomotives. Introduced in 1962, the class was responsible for powering most Paddington-Bristol-South Wales and West of England duties up to the beginning of 1977. Their performance was first class, with few failures or technical problems. The 90 mph top speed, aided by good acceleration permitted considerable time saving which greatly assisted in the development of InterCity services in the West Country.

The most powerful of the diesel-hydraulic types, the distinctive appearance of the Westerns was enhanced by cast name and number plates. After trials of differing colour schemes on the first few locomotives, nearly all were delivered in an attractive maroon livery, later appearing in standard rail blue.

Class 50

This class, although always considered part of the BR fleet when introduced in 1966/67 was, in fact, owned by English Electric Leasings, who operated a hire arrangement with BR. The fifty locomotives entered service from Crewe diesel depot and operated on the northern section of the West Coast main line. They were provided from new with electric train heating and were subsequently fitted with multiple control equipment.

The locomotives' prime work was on services between Crewe and Glasgow over the steeply graded Shap and Beattock inclines. From May 1970 Class 50s operated in pairs on the new accelerated Anglo-Scottish schedules preparing the route for high-speed electric services. When electrification was completed between Crewe and Glasgow in May 1974, the class became surplus on the London Midland Region and was moved to the Western Region to replace diesel-hydraulic locomotives. By this time the 50s were BR-owned and on the WR the fleet was allocated to Bristol, Plymouth and Old Oak Common depots and soon took over the majority of Paddington-Bristol and West of England duties. Their introduction permitted wider deployment of electrically heated coaches. The locomotives' speed of 100 mph also allowed journey time improvements on some routes.

In later years, numerous technical problems befell the class but these were rectified by a major refurbishment programme in the 1980s. Their use on Western's own InterCity services was short lived following the introduction of IC125s and the fleet was moved to inter-regional services. Subsequently, they were also replaced on Cross Country routes by IC125s and many of the class ended their days on Network SouthEast's Waterloo to Exeter route.

Class 47

The largest fleet of diesel locomotives associated with InterCity, is the Brush/BR-built Type 4 Class 47s. Over 500 were built between 1963 and 1967 for main line passenger and freight work. The fleet operated to virtually all parts of the BR network, and was associated with the development of many InterCity routes. No. D1733 was used with the prototype XP64 train, and was the first main-line diesel painted in BR blue. When introduced the first batch of locomotives was fitted with dual steam/electric heating but the majority was only fitted for steam heating.

During December 1987, with the allocation of locomotives to BR business units, a batch of Class 47s was allocated to InterCity. Many of these were modified with extended fuel tanks to increase their operating range, and were maintained for full 95 mph operation.

At the end of 1993, InterCity's long range Class 47s were responsible for powering most non - IC125 diesel services ranging from overnight Sleepers to Cross Country trains. A number of Class 47s were also used on InterCity infrastructure duties.

Class 44/45/46

These three similar classes were known as the 'Peak' type as the original locomotives – Class 44 built in 1959 – were named after British hills and mountain. The main production services was Class 45 designed principally for main line passenger duties. They were the mainstay of the Midland main line from the early 1960s and were also allocated to Bristol, working many cross-country trains. After IC125s became the InterCity power on the Midland main line, the Class 45s operated additional long-distance cross-country services such as those between Scotland and Penzance, as well as duties on the Trans Pennine corridor.

The final batch of 'Peaks', the Class 46s, were introduced from 1961 and were originally allocated to Derby and Gateshead for cross-country and East Coast work. Later the Class 46s became the regular power for cross-country duties, eventually being allocated to Laira and Gateshead depots.

Class 42/43

These two classes, introduced from 1958 onwards, were more usually referred to as Warships since most were named after Royal Navy vessels and were the production version of Class 41. The two classes – 42 built by BR and 43 by the North British Locomotive Company – were the mainstay of the Western Region's main line diesel fleet, along with the Class 52s, until the early 1970s. The Warships were rostered for the majority of Paddington to the West of England duties and for many years powered services such as the 'Cornish Riviera Express', 'Royal Duchy' and 'Mayflower.' The classes also featured largely on cross-country services, which took them to Birmingham and, during the mid-1960s, as far north as Crewe. In common with all locomotives designed during the 1950s, steam heating and vacuum brakes were fitted. As modern air-braked, electrically-heated stock was introduced, the Warships were transferred to other duties. Their appearance was based on the technically similar V200 class of DB, the West German railway. The locomotives were finally withdrawn in 1972.

Class 41

The five locomotives forming this pioneering diesel-hydraulic class were used on principal London to Plymouth and Penzance services from their introduction in 1958. They were the first express passenger diesel locomotives resulting from the 1955 Modernisation Plan to enter service. By the time InterCity was launched in 1966 they had been reduced to secondary duties. However, they deserve inclusion here as they played a major role in the modernisation of the Western Region, paving the way for the London-Penzance dieselisation programme. These locomotives were named after famous Royal Navy vessels – a theme which was followed by the production fleets (classes 42/43).

A smaller version of this locomotive, Class 22 (pictured right), was of similar appearance and was also introduced onto the Western Region to begin the transition from steam to diesel.

Class 40

The Class 40 fleet of diesel-electric locomotives, first introduced in 1958, was for many years the mainstay of the London Midland, Eastern and Scottish Region's long-distance services.

During the late 1960s and 1970s the class was gradually replaced on prime InterCity duties but up to their final withdrawal in 1988 examples could still be found at the head of InterCity expresses. The Class 40s were stalwart performers on express duties and very reliable locomotives, powering a diversity of InterCity duties from Anglo-Scottish expresses to cross-country services.

The early versions incorporated corridor connections in the 'nose ends' for crew-change purposes although, as with other classes fitted with them, they were soon taken out of use.

Class 37

This sizeable fleet of over 300 locomotives, built from 1960 through to the time of the 1966 InterCity launch, was one of BR's most successful designs. Over the years the fleet worked to virtually all corners of the BR system, powering almost every type of train. In InterCity use, Class 37s operated many duties on the Liverpool Street-Norwich/Yarmouth route, in the North West, Scotland and Wales. In 1965 two locomotives took part in high-speed trials on the Western Region between Paddington and Plymouth.

When built, Class 37s were fitted with steam-heating equipment only, and as trains became electrically-heated this reduced Class 37 locomotives' availability for passenger work. During 1985-86 a batch of thirty one Class 37s formed part of a major refurbishment programme contracted to BREL Crewe, after which the class was used for main line passenger work, mainly in the North and Scotland. Following sectorisation, the bulk of Class 37s was taken over for freight and departmental use. By May 1992 a batch of nine locomotives was allocated to the InterCity business for overnight duties in Scotland.

Class 31

One of the first main line diesel locomotive classes to emerge from the 1955 Modernisation Plan, the versatile Class 31s have stood the test of time and many are still in use today.

Introduced in 1958, a total of 263 were delivered and have been employed in all parts of the country except Scotland. They were generally used on medium distance passenger services and for freight haulage. With the allocation of rolling stock to railway business a small number were allocated to InterCity to haul maintenance trains for the infrastructure function.

INDEX

Bold figures indicate photographs

April 1994 – A new era dawns for InterCity